# COLLEGE *ACCELERATION*

Innovating Through the New American Research High School

# ERIC J. BAN

*For Information:*

Elephant Rock Productions, Inc.
Elephant Rock Books, Imprint
PO Box 119
Ashford, CT 06278
www.erpmedia.net/books

Forum On Education
www.forumoneducation.org

Printed in the United States of America

First Edition

10  9  8  7  6  5  4  3  2  1

Library of Congress Control Number: 2011939539

ISBN: 978-0-9846700-0-0

| | |
|---|---|
| Publisher | Jotham Burrello |
| Forum Director | Leonard C. Burrello |
| Copy Editor | Daniel Prazer |
| Book Design | Mollie Johanson |
| Typesetter | Fisheye Graphic Services |

# CONTENTS

# PREFACE

FROM BUSINESS EXECUTIVE TO EDUCATIONAL LEADER

*"Poetry is what gets lost in translation."*

ROBERT FROST

### Business to Education: Not Lost in Translation, February 2008

From the thirty-eighth floor of the Chase Tower in a corporate office in downtown Dallas, I gazed over my computer screen out the window to watch the Southwest Airlines 737s make a beeline for Love Field. The planes were like clockwork, coming in every thirty minutes from Houston. Welcome to the Texas-style commuter train. The planes seemed so close, yet the building was so well insulated that I could not hear or feel any noise or vibrations. In my confined and comfortable corporate setting, I smelled the expensive leather office chairs, glimpsed the hand-selected paintings down the hallways, and pictured the sculptures that guided you into a boardroom with windows that looked over the entire arts district in downtown Dallas. The view from the top of corporate America is impressive, but I was a couple months away from a huge transition from corporate America to public education, and my senses seemed to be more aware of my surroundings. I knew it was time to just brainstorm the list, just to get started writing. I had never been a high school principal before—though I had served as an assistant principal for three years in a large high school in Bloomington, Indiana. I was about to return to the Hoosier state to lead one of the largest comprehensive high schools in the state, Crown Point High School.

I opened a new file on my computer. *"Let's see, how about time chunks like the first thirty, sixty, ninety days? What is reasonable to get done in that timeframe?"*

In no order of importance, I jotted down my leadership to-do list. These things seemed critical sitting one floor below the Petroleum Club, the famous haunt where JR Ewing did all his big deals years ago on the TV series *Dallas*.

### The Leadership List:

* Develop clear roles and responsibilities for school's administration team
* Evaluation of and planning for school budget
* Construct portrait of a CPHS graduate with community
* Develop comprehensive CPHS communication plan for summer
* Construct comprehensive CPHS summer calendar
* Train leadership team on program evaluation and quality tools
* Develop a school brand and graphics standards
* Reinvent the school Website
* Develop professional community norms with entire faculty
* Develop theme with entire faculty
* Develop new teacher orientation and induction program for CPHS
* Business community forums to shape business partnership criteria
* Parent community forums to shape parent organization
* College partnership: dual credit conversations
* ACT partnership: assessment items and dual credit exam study

→ Indiana Governor's Office state support

→ Identification of instructional technology backbone for future

→ Student forums to shape student leadership initiatives

→ Individual teacher meetings to introduce myself

→ Plan and execute instructional leadership retreat for department chairs

→ Meet with school improvement team

→ Begin articulation planning with middle schools

→ Construct Teacher Leadership Academy proposal

There are so many well-documented leadership and management skills that are important. There is one skill, however, that stands above all. I didn't really grasp it until I was in private industry. What you don't focus on makes the difference! For example, why not place all maintenance and custodial operations at the high school with my athletic department. I could not waste an ounce of learning leadership time on building operations. My assistant principal team would not touch or deal with anything other than programming to help kids directly.

> **n. FROM BUSINESS TO EDUCATIONAL LEADERSHIP TRANSLATION 1**
>
> What you don't focus on is vital to your success in both business and education.

A close second, and equally as vital leadership skill, is in developing a culture of innovation: fishing with multiple poles. If you have networks, know you need partners, you need to continuously cast your lines in the water and work them. Don't throw the line in the water if your pole is a "don't focus on" pole. Carefully select poles and work the lines that are completely aligned to the focus you have established.

> **n. FROM BUSINESS TO EDUCATIONAL LEADERSHIP TRANSLATION 2**
>
> Fish with multiple poles aligned to a strategic plan. Not every pole will hit, but when one does that is completely aligned with your vision, reel it in, baby!

Thus, the list was very important to generate in order to know which poles to cast into the water.

I often find myself talking about my business experience to people outside of education. The phrase that we need more "business people" in education is spoken often in economic and political circles. Besides these folks connecting with the vocabulary I brought with me from my corporate experience, I asked myself two leadership questions:

1. What is it about my business experience that has really translated into helping me be a good leader in an educational setting?

2. How can my business experience help me connect the dots of civic and economic development, post-secondary education and training, and K-12 education?

I set the principal list aside for a moment and reflected on how I had landed in the Dallas business world in January 2005. I left a position as a visiting professor at Indiana University to move out of state for the first time. Luckily, the dean of education at Indiana told me I needed to get the hell out of the academic world and go build things. I was a builder of programs—not a university type. I had always been the odd man out who fit in mostly because I was pretty good at being one of the guys. I had always been a great number two (assistant coach, assistant principal, assistant professor, etc.). I believe most people went along with me because I was either a nice guy and/or I was relentless and would just not go away. Regardless, I always had a way of getting unexpectedly good things done, so I am told.

After being a teacher, assistant principal, and professor, I had entered the corporate world of an educational startup company. This world was lead by a brilliant entrepreneur and executive team that would push me to the brink and back. You can fall down in a competitive and relentless environment, but not for long. In any new position there are intense times of doubt and question. I hit the wall many times, but I found myself embracing the expectations and enjoying the hunt.

In my first year, I was handed an expense account and a mission to find the most powerful practices that bridged the gap between high school, college, and the workplace. In fact, in the early days, the working title for one of our startup companies was College High School (CHS). My schedule made me a frequent visitor to Love Field as well as the Dallas/Fort Worth airport: fly to Utah to look at pioneers of dual credit; fly to Florida to look at pioneers of online high schools; fly to Napa Valley to look at pioneers of one-to-one technology and project-based learning environments; fly to Denver to meet with leaders in learning management systems; fly to Boston and get smarter; fly to Austin and get even smarter where the weather, food, and music grip you like a homerun hitter grips his bat. Not only did I get to fly out and meet the best minds in the country, I also helped to bring in the best minds in the country to meet in the boardroom of the thirty-eighth floor of the Chase Tower. We would systematically learn and share, and then we would go up to the

**n.** FROM BUSINESS TO EDUCATIONAL LEADERSHIP TRANSLATION 3

Hiring bright people with a can-do attitude is hiring bright people with a can-do attitude. I don't see barriers like licensure that many see in education. I see opportunities for people to inspire kids to perform and have enough experience and intellect to learn what they need to learn to be effective. Teachers are now "intervention specialists." I want people that can bring me solutions. In business, we didn't want people too entrenched in their ways that they could not see new ways of producing better results. Thus, I look for workers, thinkers, team players, and people who have a great combination of self-assurance and humility. Give me an dreamer who can produce!

Petroleum Club for lunch—a uniquely Dallas experience where the wealthy ghosts of old white oil men hover amongst the six-figure paintings on the wall. Often our systematic learning would really just be a job interview, and we hired bright people who, like us, wanted to change the world. At times we hired so many top executives that the officer's club got a bit full. Remember, when you go to battle, soldiers are critical as well.

Imagine that you were able to take a year just to learn about the best ideas in the country in one specific area—how to help more kids succeed in the transition from high school to college, the workplace, and life. What if you then got paid well to learn this? Most people are lucky to carve out a small sliver of time and energy to think about innovation. My whole world was invention. I was able to dream, apply my understandings, and develop model after model to change the world of education for the better. Every idea was torn apart, and some concepts began to stick. The big idea was to effectively accelerate college in high school. We were inventing a way to wholesale college inside of high schools, using the most innovative and emerging learning theories and technologies available.

American high schools are irrelevant in so many ways. Reading scores actually decline over time for huge numbers of high school students. Kids are placed in tracks where they stay until the bitter end, and compliance is the main goal for many leaders. This understanding fuels a passion to drive significant change. When you are at the nexus of building the breakthrough educational company that will change the world, you suddenly find yourself surrounded by people who think like you. I realized I was part of a movement. I realized that I would now drive hard with some of the brightest people I had ever met until we produced results.

### The Boardroom: You're Fired!

People work in jobs and they create a self-image and identity around a specific role (a teacher, a policeman, an accountant). In a start-up company, you are a piece on the chessboard. You are lucky to be on the board; you take risks and work to gain equity and work politically to develop some sense of security and better placement on the board. In my educational startup, I served in so many roles. I had at least ten business cards in my desk. At times I was the professor from Indiana, the former high school administrator, the chemistry teacher who taught university courses to high school students, the skipper, the professor, but never the millionaire.

The boardroom is a crazy place. There are so many different experiences there:

* Serious meetings where you are challenged to think at a moments notice and contribute something of value, or you run the risk of not returning.
* Brainstorming sessions where the floor is open to ideas.
* Vision meetings, where the big boss brings you in to sell you on a big vision. (He is working you over to see if his own people will bite on a new idea.)
* Business meetings with other enterprises, where you are challenged to joust and outmaneuver your adversaries in negotiations.

**n. FROM BUSINESS TO EDUCATIONAL LEADERSHIP TRANSLATION 4**

Everything is about promoting ideas. As an educational leader, you are constantly sharing your ideas one student, one parent, one teacher, one business leader, and one school board member at a time. My principal's conference room became the board room. Expulsion, vendor sales, teacher cancellation of contracts, strategy sessions. All these board room experiences apply, and they all begin and end in action! Educational leadership programs need to throw candidates over to the business school for sales and marketing training.

→ Company sales meetings, where you are part of a team to establish credibility and develop commitments from another group.

→ Interviews where you are required to lock in people and gain commitment.

→ Sales meetings where you have to practice your pitch to sell your product in front of the senior leadership of the company for critique.

In the boardroom, the scoreboard is always on—what have you done for me lately? Every box score is posted, every move is transparent, and every player is exposed. These are the conditions that hunters like. I have found that business people typically behave like hunters, and education people typically behave like gatherers. The wiring is just different due to the purpose being different. Mostly, in business, no matter how mission-driven you are, it all comes down to shareholders and money. This bottom line drives a more aggressive orientation in business leadership. In education, no matter how you slice it, the bottom line is customer satisfaction. This bottom line drives a more caring and compassionate educational leadership. Thus, the way that dinner is placed on the table is different. With all that said, the boardroom is for company leadership, and most folks in an emerging company don't spend much time there at all. For the folks building and implementing in the field, the world takes on a bit more of a normal sense. But if you want to be on the scoreboard in business, you need to perform effective hunting moves in the boardroom.

In the spring of 2006, I was in Chicago in the boardroom of one of the colleges we owned. I was leading many initiatives and running programs. We dramatically changed learning models for our master's degree students at least three times in a twelve-month period. When I say changed learning models, I mean really changed learning models, like requiring satellite dishes on the top of schools to giving all master's students a laptop. The students were great sports, and as I look back on our work, we were actually modeling innovation for our master's students. They had to adapt, adjust, and perform—true twenty-first century skills. In the midst of managing the student expectations and solving problems for the college, our brilliant entrepreneur turned to me and said that I wasn't capable of developing product and that I was going into sales. The funny thing was I wasn't developing product at the time. Hey, I just got moved on the chessboard, and was lucky to still be on the board. I remember walking out of the meeting and turning to a colleague to say, "I just got fired from a job I didn't even have."

My friend and colleague just smiled and said I could put my product development business card away for a while. I felt like Uncle Billy in *It's a Wonderful Life* when George told him he could take a string off his finger. Hey, I still retained nine business cards!

> **FROM BUSINESS TO EDUCATIONAL LEADERSHIP TRANSLATION 5**
>
> Twenty-first century skills that play in all environments from the top brass to the individual students we served in our master's programs:
> - Adaptability
> - Productivity
> - Teamwork
> - Professional Attitude
>
> These have made our master's students great leaders for twenty-first century learning environments.

In Dallas, I received the professional blessing we all seek. I found my professional space in education with other folks who loved to hunt and who had track records of killing lots of game. This educational startup was the place that helped a group of hunters use our collective experiences to truly open up our gifts. It is Christmas morning every day in a startup. If you have seen the movie *Groundhog Day*, where the main character, played by Bill Murray, relives the title's holiday over and over, you will soon realize that having Christmas and opening gifts every day has issues. You get bloated on stuffing and fruit cake, visit uncomfortably with relatives you don't know all that well,

Six years after beginning the work in Dallas, I am proud of the companies that emerged from Best Associates to serve the world with more affordable, accessible, and accountable higher education. I am consistently amazed at the resolve and intensity of my former colleagues and the new rock stars they consistently attract.

Hunters dream about hunting. I enjoy talking to my friends and colleagues on a weekly basis. They share the latest strategy to recruit students, manage customer relations, reduce the cost of producing courseware, etc. I love to learn, and I love to hunt.

and the cleanup of the wrapping paper and dishes is not something you look forward to everyday. Sometimes you just long to have a pizza delivered.

### Back Home Again: The Hunter in the Corn Field

In June, 2008, it was time to go back home and settle into something stable with my family where I grew up, thirty miles southeast of Chicago, just over the Illinois border, in Northwest Indiana. I was a Merrillville High School graduate and our archrival in basketball was Crown Point. We had knock down, drag out basketball battles. At my first school board meeting, I was met with a blown up picture from a newspaper story twenty years earlier of me driving against a Crown Point player in real short basketball shorts. The headline clearly promoted a Crown Point win. I had a 5-1 record against Crown Point in my Junior and Senior year, but they happened to find a picture from the only loss (I am modestly competitive, in case you haven't noticed). Soon after, I accepted the job and moved back to Indiana to take the helm at Crown Point High School. The people were awesome and the vision was right, but it still felt as if I were being hired by the old phone company when I had new mobile phone technology skill sets. Wow, at times it seemed like I had machine gun standing alone in a cornfield. What skills did I learn in Dallas that could help me lead this new work in a traditional suburban high school? In additional to the aforementioned leadership, two big ideas emerged during target practice.

*Relationships: A network of great minds.* I lived in Bloomington, Indiana, for sixteen years. Indiana University provided me the opportunity as a teacher, administrator, and professor to interact with some of the best minds in the country. A powerhouse Research I institution, as defined by the Carnegie Foundation, however, paled in comparison to my corporate experience at Best Associates where I worked alongside world leaders in education, technology, policy, business, and multinational corporations. I have strong relationships because I worked hard to support folks across all our company ventures. When I have a question or idea, I pick up the phone and call some of the best minds in the world. If you are to lead in education, it is no different from business—you have to get out there and build a just-in-time intellectual network.

*Understandings: Big vision and no barriers.* The first step of the big vision is a powerful and almost unrealistic belief system. My belief is that all students can succeed in post-secondary education and training with the right combination of opportunities and supports. I'd just finished a four-year tour to reinvent higher education for the world in a grueling startup environment; I had to believe that it could actually happen. I had worked on launching companies and products that attempted to drive motivation, develop skills, and instill work ethic in our students. These three things can do amazing things for our society.

At least ninety percent of the education people I talk to place false barriers up because of low expectations and a history of entrenched behavior. The big secret to serving all kids well is to not pigeonhole the kids or the work. You can't be elitist for the "Advanced Placement" kids; you can't be for only job training and marginalize the "vocational kids." All kids means *all kids*. How do you become the school that provides meaningful and relevant programming and supports for all students? It is pretty simple concept—start with workforce development (the emerging best jobs), work backwards with your post-secondary partners (universities, trade organizations, community colleges), and lay out a sequence of experiences that provides college equivalents with twenty-first century skills to all students, a sort of running start into post-high school life. The concept is simple, but the execution is brutal, because no one has the boardroom experience to negotiate and execute the mergers, joint ventures, and takeovers that need to occur to get it done. This is the work I had to figure out coming back to the traditional high school. What is the model and policy environment to *really* connect the dots between secondary and post-secondary? Many of the new models of high schools out there are tough to scale with little empirical evidence of effectiveness.

At first I could not articulate all the dimensions of this transformation effectively. I was challenged to define a new type of institution of secondary/ post-secondary learning (the research high school). Next, I had to figure out a way for innovations to translate practice across a network of high schools. Finally, I had to figure out how to link of this new work to regional economic and civic development. Once I began to create this concept with colleagues in my school, region, state, and across the country I soon realized my boardroom experience had to emerge—sales! People will not buy what they don't understand, so I knew I would have to spend a ridiculous amount of time on marketing the big vision of college and career acceleration for all kids with the research high school, network and economic development. All kids can achieve post-secondary success with R & D investment in our best schools.

I have not sat under the paintings in the Petroleum Club for a few years where I was building models to transform education and make money. In my new role, I have consistently sustained my drive to help the institution of the American public high school re-establish a prominent role in the world economy through college and workforce acceleration!

**_n._ FROM BUSINESS TO EDUCATIONAL LEADERSHIP TRANSLATION 6**

Invest in your best opportunities. Education often invests in the worst school environments. This deficit planning and investment is a huge barrier for the growth of the institution of the American public high school.

For business leaders, the new American Research High School is the equivalent to a research hospital, a place where new practices are expected and tested. It is this R & D function that is so valued in business and is so clearly missing in education. It is a place where business leaders consistently challenge educators to produce a new twenty-first century worker to lead a new American economy. It is a place where education shifts from deficit planning in our worst schools to opportunity planning in our best schools. Here in the research high school, we invest in our future. These investments produce new models of practice that produce new results. As in health care, these new practices move out quickly through systems and networks so everyone produces new results, and America can rise in world rankings in post-secondary attainment and in economic development. R & D investment ultimately generates revenue to revitalize communities, regions, states, and the country!

R&D → HUMAN CAPITAL → NEW COMPANIES → STRONGER ECONOMY/ REGION → NEW REVENUE

For educators, the new American Research High School is a collaborative professional learning environment where teachers, students, and parents work with focus and transparency to individualize a plan for success for every student. The research high school is not for all teachers as the research hospital is not for all doctors. Teachers consistently ask tough questions to challenge current practices and construct new models in partnership with vendors, universities, state departments, and regional leaders to help all students achieve beyond their potential. Teachers who choose to do this work have time, like research faculty at a hospital, and they have an intense responsibility to their practice to develop scalable models that can be translated across the practice.

University professors may be asking what is the difference between the classic university "lab school" and the new American Research High School? The answer is very simple. The research high school is driven by regional economic development and has oversight by regional industry leaders. These leaders are the pillars of regional stability; they have run time tested successful businesses, and they understand the needs of the regional work force as well as the civic agenda. Universities should definitely be a part of the work of research high schools, but there is one clear purpose here, and that is college and workforce readiness and success. Millions of students in the United States are not college and workforce ready when they receive their high school diploma, and this is our clear agenda: *College Acceleration!*

Back in Dallas I packed up my toolkit of networks, boardroom experience, conscious ignorance, and my fishing poles. And soon after I scribbled out my list of goals I hopped a Southwest 737 north to Indiana and began building a *The New American Research High School* dedicated to college and workforce readiness with a talented and committed community, district leadership team, administrative team, faculty, parents, and students. This book documents our three-year journey.

ERIC J. BAN, SEPTEMBER 2011

## PERSONAL COMMENT

Six months after moving to Crown Point, I sat with my father and watched my son hit a game-winning three point shot in a seventh grade basketball game. People asked me why I left corporate America and walked away from all that money? Buying a coat for Chicagoland? 150 bucks. Buying a new video camera to tape my son's games? 300 bucks. Sitting next to grandpa when his grandson hits the game winning shot? Priceless! I have been blessed to do this work in the context of my roots and family.

# PART I

CREATING URGENCY

*"The voyage of discovery is not in seeking
new landscapes but in having new eyes."*

MARCEL PROUST

# Chapter One

When you enter the world of the traditional phone company and you have been working on mobile device technology for years, it presents a real dilemma. How do I help people realize that we can get better results here? How do I help people realize that even in suburbia we have a long way to go? How do I help the seemingly most successful people in the most nurturing setting in the most confident country in the world recognize the urgency for change? I thought about what makes great schools and I landed on values. So we went back to basics with the kids and community.

It took twenty minutes to get all 2,500 students into the home stands of the football stadium on the first day of the school year in the fall of 2008. I was sweating, and not necessarily from the heat. What was I doing? The newspapers, the school board, the superintendent, and folks came out to see what we were doing. I felt like Gene Hackman in *Hoosiers* when he began to run a ball-controlled offense. How dare I take away class time for this frivolous assembly stuff? I had worked all summer with the leadership team and the entire community to re-establish the values of our community. At the completion of that work, a question lingered: how do you re-introduce a community to itself? I stepped to the center of the field and I picked up the microphone. My voice boomed over the loudspeaker. "We will come back into these stands at the end of the year, and one of you will be handed the keys to this." A new, red 2009 Chevy Cobalt rolled out on the track and parked in front of the student body. The kids were stunned. I always think a pleasantly stunned class is a good situation for a teacher. You get one chance to make a first impression. Go big!

The car was the big prize for the new "Ticket to Ride" C-Note program. The C-Note program was at the heart of our school-wide Positive Behavioral Intervention Supports, or PBIS. This new incentive system was designed as a whole school climate and cultural system to increase positive behaviors toward valued goals for each student in the school. This program re-introduced a community to its values. The system was designed with a number of positive behaviors as goals and incentives that catch kids doing things right. The desired end results or values (the six Cs) were developed over the summer with our parents, kids, faculty, and our leadership team. The real opportunity it presented was to know which kids were not engaged at Crown Point High School. It was an opportunity to see that when kids demonstrated our values through actions, they did better with their grade point average and increased their college readiness as measured by our ACT tools.

Over the stadium loudspeakers, I explained to the students how to win a C-Note by demonstrating the newly established values of the school community:

- College: Honor roll
- Career: Perfect attendance
- Citizenship: Community and school service
- Creativity: Club or student activity participation
- Courage: Sports participation and standing up for something
- Culture: Art and performing arts participation

And so the race for the car began. Students racked up C-Notes all year as we promoted the positive behaviors through videos, parking the Chevy Cobalt in the front circle drive, playing the Beatles "Ticket to Ride" over the intercom. At the end of the year, we had over 10,000 "tickets to ride," or C-Notes, in a giant bingo bin. Again, we assembled the student body in the football bleachers, and I pulled the winning ticket out. It belonged to a deserving sophomore girl who had good grades, good attendance, club participation, played in the orchestra, and ran cross-country—she happened to be the ideal portrait of a CPHS student. Sometimes a plan comes together.

### *Suburbia's Little Secret: Disengagement—the Forgotten Middle*

Schools often hide behind their numbers. We had a great school in the eyes of most people, but we, like many schools had our little secret in the suburbs—disengagement. So just as the data showed who was connected, it showed who was not. The data told us that we had a problem of disengaged students. In a school of 2,500 students, twenty-five percent of the student body did not receive a C-Note toward our valued outcomes in the 2008-2009 school year. I opened up the yearbook and counted every picture that had only one number by the name (which indicated that there was only one place to find this student in the yearbook—the school picture). Twenty five percent of the students in the yearbook were literally just a face at Crown Point High School. I counted how many kids failed Algebra that year—twenty-five percent. This was a problem—that's 750 disengaged kids! How can an exemplary high school, a designation we received for the first time ever that same year, have herds of students living inside our building not engaged in demonstrating our values? Suddenly, we had a new way of diagnosing symptoms—the symp-

---

**NOTE**

As a professor at Indiana University, I worked on the High School Survey of Student Engagement (HSSSE). This was fun and ground breaking work that began to provide schools data on student perceptions and actions related to their engagement. Students reported on time spent on homework, perceptions of relevance, involvement in school activities. This data picture was very new for many high schools and proved to be a catalyst for many schools to act!

---

tom of disengagement. We do have an urgent cause in suburban America: to eradicate disengagement.

We kept track of every student who didn't earn a C-Note. I printed out a list of all those kids and hung it in the mailroom, and every adult in the building was challenged to adopt a kid. We reduced the number of students not receiving a C-Note by five percent the first year, and five more the second year. That equates to 250 more kids with C-Notes, or symbols of demonstrating our values. Pretty soon we will eradicate disengagement through strong programming and relationships. It was time to get it done the right way and get out of the car give-away business. We need, as Phil Schlechty and Michael Fullan have argued, intrinsic student motivation to guide engagement and participation in all aspects of school life.

The leaders of corporate America live in suburbia. The traditional suburban high school serves the needs of their already well-served kids. Their image is important in the most confident country in the world. As NCLB begins to label their schools as failing, NCLB will be quietly whisked away like the mimeograph machine after Xerox developed the copier. There are too many problems with the current federal accountability picture for high schools. High schools are a complicated animal for oversimplified state accountability systems to be applied in a fair and relevant way. Corporate and political leaders will redirect the focus and embrace a new acronym to beat up urban education, and the cycle of reform that ignores suburbia will continue indefinitely.

Much of the accountability picture in education is flawed from a simple standpoint that it works from a deficit model. If you are working with corporate hunter types, they can handle deficit leadership. You dish out punishment to them, and they go take that aggression out by killing something and landing a big sale. When you work with gatherer types in education, they don't respond so well to taking a beating in the paper. Most gatherers (and hunters for that matter) respond much better to building on strengths. Just look at most of the successful self-help programs. I believe that my awareness to work from people's strengths has been a powerful realization in my work at the school. We have talented people who know they have to grow and improve. The way we get better is to use data, be inclusive and in the most collaborative way, turn on the scoreboard for teams of people to win together. Good school people will play the game hard if it is fair and team oriented. Good hunters are actually more effective when they take down game in packs as well.

### PERSPECTIVE

The No Child Left Behind Act attempted to generate a sense of urgency by requiring school districts to measure student achievement data by subgroups (traditionally underperforming groups, students of color, English language learners, and those with disabilities). Suburban America continued to skirt the issue with traditionally compliant kids from typically higher socio-economic groups who generally performed adequately on minimum competency expectations. Let's review our accountability system adjectives: generally, adequately, minimum; *Let's all Race to the Top with these words.*

### *Less Complicated?—Learn From Elementary Schools*

Our work on identifying disengaged kids was a nice way to think about serving kids better, but it was only part of the equation. We had to revisit a key purpose of our work and find some instruments to help us look at data. I have watched the elementary school principals' work with grade level teams on growth data, formative math and reading data, professional learning community processes, and manageable school size to build a sense of family and community. I really get jealous when I see this good work taking place all over the country. Many large high schools, on the other hand, continue as complex beasts that have eaten up billions of dollars of foundation and federal money with very few sustainable reforms and results.

The Crown Point community recognized that a new set of measurement instruments was required if we were going to actually drive the college and workforce readiness results; we needed to deliver on our mission for all kids to be college and career ready. We embraced ACT tools and began to assess college readiness skills in every eighth-grade student through their junior year. We needed to see a longitudinal picture of student growth on math, science, reading, and English. We began to ignore the state assessment game due to irrelevance of the minimum competency expectations and questionable state standards. We could play the Indiana high school assessment game well with our clientele, but to what end? The ACT system began to come together to help us look at our results on college readiness. This created a second call to action. The percentage of our sophomore students reading at college readiness benchmarks actually decreased (it's not uncommon for reading levels to decrease in high schools).

A data picture began to emerge and was slowly and carefully shared with the faculty. It helped us revisit the purpose of schooling. We surveyed the faculty on our direction, asking about valuing college and career-readiness. The survey data was overwhelmingly positive, but the data was overwhelmingly shocking: disengagement and lack of real college readiness. The data strategy was not hard—moving at the speed of faculty buy-in and trust, as identified by Stephen M.R. Covey, is another story. Building professional trust was the next hurdle in creating the foundation for the New American Research High School.

# Chapter Two

*"The first responsibility of a leader is to define reality.*
*The last is to say thank you."*

MAX DEPREE

### One Person, One Heart at a Time

Urgency is panic unless there is trust. When I came to the school in the summer of 2008, before my first school year, I scheduled thirty-minute conversations with all 115 faculty members in their classrooms. The last place I wanted to introduce myself to the faculty was in the principal's office. (How pompous would that be?) I wanted to learn about people, focus, traditions, and passion. Where did the faculty want this thing to go? I crafted a script. (I am a maniac on preparation and consistency—my research training kicks in constantly thanks to my doctoral experience). The conversations were driven by the following prompts:

- ⇥ Tell me a little bit about you and what you do here at Crown Point?
- ⇥ What moment did you know you were in the right place?
- ⇥ How will you know when you reach the top of your profession?
- ⇥ What are some of the barriers that stand in the way of reaching the top of your profession here at Crown Point?

- ↦ What time-honored traditions make Crown Point special and just should not be touched?

- ↦ What would you throw out tomorrow if you could, because it is not good for kids?

- ↦ Give me three words or themes that will help Crown Point become the best it can be?

- ↦ What expertise do you offer to your colleagues who may need support?

- ↦ Where do you need support to improve your instructional practices for the benefit of kids?

- ↦ What would you like to know about me and about my commitment to support you?

## LEADERSHIP

I could list hundreds of authors and books, but I use this simple concept from the late Bill Foster to challenge those in our school to be critical leaders:

Critical Leadership (Foster, 1989) adapted for CPHS strategic planning:

Critical: *"Best"* leaders always challenge current practice and develop a culture of risk-taking

Educative: *"Best"* leaders learn intensely about research, standards, best practice, and community needs

Transformative: *"Best"* leaders inspire people to act and get results (beliefs change with results)

Ethical: *"Best"* leaders model and protect community agreements while working towards a clear moral purpose

I kept meticulous notes on the faculty input so I clearly understood individual and collective perspectives and ideas. Every school leader knows that the school moves at the speed of faculty trust, and in a school the size of Crown Point, this is a really tough goal to pursue. I knew that I could build some positive energy and get some folks to take steps with me, but the long haul is built on capacity. The faculty had to see an administrative team, not a just a principal. The faculty had to work in departments where the chairs are strong and supportive. The faculty had to individually and collectively produce big results for kids, and the parents and students had to become more engaged and see the work in a very transparent way. We could not let one ounce of mediocrity exist in the school, so I knew I had to be very diligent on moving folks out of some key seats. Yes, our leadership team read *Good to Great* by Jim Collins. We started to get the right people in the right seats quickly. The appropriate questions for leaders are how do you engage, build trust, and drive hard?

### *Community Agreements*

If you were to survey a large comprehensive high school faculty on their needs, the last thing on the list would be a set of professional agreements to guide adult behavior. These secondary people are thick-skinned folks. We roll a bit differently in large high schools. The teacher in the classroom is king, and all else around them is fluff. As a new principal, I had to have some firepower behind addressing poor adult behavior other than me playing dad. We took a few faculty meetings and did some survey work to establish a set of professional agreements that we revisit each year. I appreciate the willingness of most of the faculty to develop these agreements. The agreements are, simply stated:

- Respect each other
- Listen without judgment
- Demonstrate trust and loyalty
- Demonstrate integrity
- Openly communicate
- Have fun

We made posters and hung them in every classroom and every hallway. Meetings start with reviewing our professional agreements as well. When folks operate outside of the agreements, I use the agreements to call out those behaviors—hey, the community has spoken. Does this always work? Absolutely not! It works well enough to help add to the culture of professionalism folks deserve. So yes, it is worth the time and energy.

Many times I will use surveys as a tool to set expectations. If you include questions about following the community agreements, it may be the first time some of the faculty actually read them. Also, I send out all our deficiencies in all their glory. There is nothing like a good crisis to generate some urgency to get something done. If we have a problem, I send it out there for all to see so we can fix it together.

Oh yeah, don't forget to survey the faculty on questions like, "Am I following the community agreements?" and, by department, "Is my department following the community agreements?" then list those agreements right there in the survey question. Now, if the answers unmask some deep-seated bad blood about staff relationships, send it out anyway; let people see that we have work to do together. Trust is established through saying how you will work together, assessing it, asking folks if we're there yet, and doing things to get there, like thanking courageous colleagues that keep others in check and removing folks that just are not healthy professionals. This is tough work that sucks the life out of leaders. Recognize the value of this work and hold the line on professionalism.

### Faculty Beliefs

The faculty is the real author of high schools in a community. Every parent and student knows which teacher they want for which course. The work of teachers is extremely public, and community trust is built through the good work and communication of a faculty. They are the core technology of the high school (teaching and learning inside classrooms). Every new concept or idea in high school has to recognize that faculty work with students is the core.

The faculty of a large high school has to speak with one voice on a few things, and one of them is a set of faculty beliefs. We spent a day session in small groups to discuss and develop these beliefs. This was not easy, and many of our more concrete sequential types were not so thrilled with spending an afternoon on this work. Much of leadership is selling the task and being so darn energetic, positive, and optimistic that negative folks have no real choice to be negative. I smile constantly and engage every negative person in a positive, upbeat, forward-thinking conversation. (Our faculty beliefs document did not include 21st century skills initially because we were not ready.) Be authentic in the work and have the faculty work products reflect reality. These are the faculty beliefs that are posted in every corner of the school:

- All students are unique.
- All students need an adult in the building that knows them as an individual.
- All students need a safe and inviting environment.
- All students need a goal for their future.
- All students should be responsible for their learning.
- All students need relevance and joy in their work.
- All students should think critically and communicate their thoughts clearly.
- All students should have the support they need to succeed.
- All students should become twenty-first century global citizens.

We are working on an updated set of beliefs through dialogue with students, parents, and the community. This will be a new guiding force that will be posted everywhere. Beliefs are powerful if they are used appropriately. A mentor once shared a wonderful and simple way of thinking about beliefs. He said, quite simply, that these are the things that I will resign over.

### Critical Friends

Well-respected external folks can be a wonderful addition in a school community. I use this strategy constantly to ignite some fires, help folks to reflect, and celebrate the work. I invite people to come to CPHS all the time, but I am selective about who is invited. The folks that are invited to come and visit are respected and valued by our school community.

One critical friend is a retired superintendent from Cook County, Illinois. He has been a high school math teacher, high school math department chair, high school principal, and a high school superintendent. He is tough and straight shooting. He came to the high school in year one during much of our belief work. He also came to blow up the administrative team's traditional mindset. He pushed on them without me around. He respected their work. He made them uncomfortable, but he made them more reflective by sharing his experiences in a tougher urban environment. He helped us think on strategic planning, faculty association representative conversations, and a number of things that needed to be examined at the school. The English department chair at the time had a nice way of positioning his work: "We haven't looked under all the rocks in a while." Everything needs to be examined and questioned so that we can figure out what needs attention and where to make adjustments. He was one of maybe twelve people

**CRITICAL FRIEND TOPICS**

Leadership, faculty administration relations, teaching strategies, teacher parent communication, guidance counselor work, teacher leadership, school culture and climate, rigor and relevance in classrooms, teacher student relationships.

that came to the school in year one to help pick up rocks and look underneath.

Another critical friend was a former guidance director at a nearby high school. He came in as a consultant and routinely worked with our guidance department. With limited administrative resources in a school of 2,500 students, using a respected outside critical friend to help guide meetings, partner on evaluations, intervene with complex issues of job territory, and more has been a wonderful and economically sound strategy.

You might be thinking that bringing in lots of people is a burden on your folks. High school people often work in isolation. When you position critical friends to come in and talk to faculty about their work, they are usually excited that someone is noticing. Also, when do high school people get to share practice with external professionals? This is a great exercise to help people with self-reflection. It has proven to be a successful strategy. I brought in Six Sigma management teams from industry to work with the administrative and guidance teams. These folks are experts in helping to improve process through helping people inside the system come up with their own solutions. Critical friends in the best sense help people in the system take responsibility and ownership in their work.

### No Man is an Island

I have been so lucky in my professional career to be around huge talent wherever I land. My work in Northwest Indiana has been nothing short of inspiring. Let's start where we always need to start in education, the kids. Oh my, do we have great kids at Crown Point. I love walking in and out of classrooms, hanging in the lunchroom, walking the parking lots after school, going to performances and athletic events. They perform in the classroom and everywhere else they go. In partnership with my parent leadership team, I wrote the following in the Parent Connections school newsletter that was mailed to every parent in my third year at Crown Point:

> CPHS continues to move into a more innovative and elite school category as result of:
>
> + A community that values and nurtures risk taking and innovation.
> + A parent community committed to strong attendance, academic performance, and extracurricular participation.
> + A system of high performing elementary and middle schools.
> + A business community that supports all CPHS programs.
> + A talented faculty, staff, and administrative team that has incredible work ethic.
> + A higher education community partnering with us to deliver college and technical programs inside our walls.
> + A workforce development community who will launch a workforce development office in CPHS this year.

The most powerful part of my work at Crown Point has been my working relationship with my superintendent. She knows my strengths and shortcomings. I over-communicate with her so she knows every single move and idea—which I'm sure is often frightening for her—and she provides me with guidance, tools, and the space to run hard. She has created a culture of high expectations for leaders. The district office company line is, "Yes, we can," and the other principals in the system have a friendly, professional, and competitive relationship. Remember lesson number one of leadership? *What you don't worry about is so important.* I can run hard because I deal with very few political community issues in my job due to the strong leadership at the top. I like to think that I agreed to leave the corporate world of the Petroleum Club to take the Crown Point job knowing that this would be the context of leadership in a new environment.

The context of leading is so important to understand. I am part of a great district leadership team. I often need help in personnel, budget, relationships, and so on. I call my district and local colleagues and consistently experience sincere help and support.

This leadership story is told over and over again in highly performing schools across this country. Capacity building is developed through constructing a culture of professionalism, developing explicit beliefs, helping professionals to reflect on their practice, and working in a context and system of strong leadership. These are time-tested ways of launching a ship, and I just followed the plan and used my training to move these things in place with the help and support of so many people.

## REFLECTION

As I would assume you are a leader if you are reading this book, I would ask a few simple questions to help you reflect:

→ List the names of the professionals in your inner professional circle.

→ List the strengths of the professionals in your inner professional circle.

→ Ask everyone in your inner circle to document the last three times they reached out for advice; who did they contact, what was the ask, did they act on the advice, did they follow up with a thank you?

No man is an island!

### *So Where Do We Dump This Nuclear Waste?*

Before we move into the next part of the book I wanted to share a few thoughts. If you read through the first two chapters you may get the false sense that everything is great in high school leadership land. This is not the case. There are some significant barriers for high school leaders. These barriers are not insurmountable, but they need to be shared before we talk about how to re-invent the American public high school.

A great friend of mine literally dropped out of high school because he was bored, enrolled at one of the best engineering schools in the world, and became a nuclear engineer. In this work he was driven to serve the needs of society for safe and effective placements of nuclear reactors and waste. He took great care and pride in constructing plans based on research, modeling, and strong data. These plans would inevitably hit the public political domain, and, suddenly, calculated safety risks gave way to emotional testimonies, private interests, and no one representing the underrepresented. Thus, a nuclear reactor would inevitably be built in a location that provided the most risk to the most under-represented populations despite the best engineering plans. I share this to talk about the barriers that public high schools face in mounting an effective movement towards better results for kids. In "public" education the institution of the American high school faces challenges similar to what my friend experienced as a young nuclear engineer.

As high school leaders, we are faced with an oversimplified picture of accountability due to the complexity of our work and a political landscape that is often driven by ideology and interests not aligned to the needs of kids and communities. In my experience, these two obstacles—complexity and politics—bump right up against innovation and improvement.

*Complexity:* I have been very fortunate through my travels and experiences to work on high school issues as a teacher, administrator, university professor, and educational business leader. Every high school environment has a different culture, community context, personality, size, student population, catalog of course offerings and programs, and a host of other variables. The buildings that serve fourteen through eighteen-year-olds in our country are tough nuts to crack. Bill Gates and others have invested billions of dollars in reform efforts with little sustainable results to show for it. Accountability and ranking systems are not sophisticated enough to respect these variables, thus high schools stop paying attention to much of the important work and focus on a few narrow variables based on these pressures.

There are hundreds of examples, but I will share one that we have at Crown Point. We have a choice to offer Advanced Placement psychology or dual credit psychology with Purdue University. The dual credit option provides our students Big Ten university credit for less money. The vast majority of our students attend state colleges and universities. Purdue transcripts are stronger currency for our students than Advanced Placement. Further, students who receive an A in the class also can apply that grade toward their college GPA. The state rewards schools for maximum Advanced Placement performance and national rankings heavily favor Advanced Placement. These systems are not able to understand that Purdue psychology is a better choice for our community. If we were unable to see this issue clearly for our kids, or we ignored our moral responsibility and chased the rankings, we could "look" better to our public if we offered Advanced Placement. We have made the moral and ethical choice to serve our community well. There are literally hundreds of these variables and decision points. The oversimplified accountability systems and rankings push leaders to ignore the needs of kids and communities and go for the rankings (many leaders have to get the category placement and rankings in order to keep their job). As in the nuclear reactor example, the underrepresented students who do not have parent advocates or special services feel the most

**ℜℜ  REFLECTION**

Complexity and politics often make high school leaders rethink the decision to lead these environments. I didn't sign up to manage a circus. At times it feels like I need to put on a big hat and walk around the school with a cane. Welcome to the greatest show on Earth! The American Public Circus!

Come look at the crazy legislation that requires that I build a course this year to teach kids about the risks of inhaling white out (Hey, wait a minute—they all got computers and don't even know what white out is?). Da, da, da, da, da, da, da, da, da, da...here comes the clowns!

pain of oversimplification. Most often, accountability systems reward schools for showing results with the top twenty-five percent by offering AP courses, and with the bottom twenty-five percent, for pushing struggling students over the bar to graduate.

*Politics:* The issues facing the American public high school are real. These issues are often difficult for those who are not inside of the education system to understand, due to educational jargon, the complexity of high school environments, and the noise created from political rhetoric. The confusion often plays well in the political arena. The high school can produce anything you want it to, from despair to hope. Pull whatever you want from the black box we call high schools and work it—test scores go up, inner city kids are going to college, bad teachers are entrenched, many schools are underfunded, and kids all over the world are outperforming the U.S. in math. It is such a simple political formula, and as a high school person, I'm tired of being used as a political football. I have no magic bullet to reduce the politics of education. I think the best we can do is to become better public intellectuals in the battleground of education. The newspapers only print sports, major celebrations, and despair for high schools. Part II of the book will equip you as a public intellectual to understand the major shifts of the American public high school.

# PART II

*One can never consent to creep when one feels an impulse to soar.*

Helen Keller

I am often asked to come to strategic planning sessions for groups like State Chambers of Commerce, ACT, and The Lumina Foundation. They like the fact that I have had the good fortune of traveling the world and witnessing powerful forces in action. They also like the fact that I have brought big ideas into a school environment as a practitioner in a very pragmatic way. For example, based on my experience, I worked with a talented group of regional university leaders to build a more accountable, affordable, and accessible model of dual credit that changed state policy and was featured in many articles and state and national conferences. The general focus of my participation in these strategic planning activities is to promote a more relevant and connected high school experience for students. Too many high school seniors are bored and disconnected. I always talk about moving from a holding pen to a launching pad approach in high schools. As the former commissioner of education in Texas once told me, "Kids ain't buying what we are selling anymore."

My dad was my best role model in developing my research and writing skills. He saved every thought, quote, and idea in file folders to write his books. In my twenty years in education, I have saved wonderful artifacts from students, parents, teachers, business leaders, and colleagues across the world. I have had the good fortune to build ideas and plans with such varied leaders such as Japanese inquiry math experts and presidents of South American universities, though I have found some of the most enlightening contributions have come from retired high school teachers and administrators. In their retirement, they remain tremendously reflective and insightful. I think I have been lucky to recognize the value of retired educators early on in my professional career. Thus, the following ideas on the major shifts in high schools have come from an experiential base and the contributions of many talented individuals.

I encourage all leaders to use these insights to nurture a more enlightened and intellectual public who can help move the conversation forward to build a more effective system for serving fourteen to eighteen-year-olds in the United States. As a qualifying statement, the middle section of this book is a way of thinking about how to move forward. There are ideas for solutions presented after each shift, but by no means is this book an implementation guide for American high schools. I aspire for everyone involved in civic and economic development initiatives to have a common set of understandings to think globally and act regionally for the benefit of fourteen through eighteen-year-old American students.

As a salesperson, I consistently talk to students, parents, colleagues, business, and political leaders about the work of high schools. They (all stakeholders) have to clearly understand this work to embrace it and help drive it. I have identified ten major shifts in the work of the American public high school.

An overview of these shifts is presented here, and each will be discussed in the following chapters.

| Shift | From | To |
|---|---|---|
| *Expectations* | *Expectations for some* | *Expectations for all* |
| *Targets* | *State content standards* | *College and workforce readiness* |
| *Tools* | *Technology as optional* | *Technology as central* |
| *Training* | *Teacher as worker* | *Student as worker* |
| *Relationships* | *Relationships by chance* | *Relationships by design* |
| *Leadership* | *The great man theory* | *Community building* |
| *Parents* | *Parents as observers* | *Parents as participants* |
| *Partnerships* | *Isolationist buildings* | *Strategic partnerships* |
| *Research* | *I feel* | *The research says* |
| *Innovation* | *Isolated breakthroughs* | *Innovation that spreads like wildfire* |

In the end, high schools need to meet every family and student at the door, engage them in their future, and help them realize their potential as a twenty-first century citizen. This is the new expectation of the American public high school—from holding pen to launching pad.

# CHAPTER THREE

*America's Interstate Highway System*
*"More than any single action by the government since the end*
*of the war, this one would change the face of America with straightaways,*
*cloverleaf turns, bridges, and elongated parkways. Its impact on the*
*American economy—the jobs it would produce in manufacturing and*
*construction, the rural areas it would open up—was beyond calculation."*

DWIGHT D. EISENHOWER *MANDATE FOR CHANGE 1953-1956* (1963)

There will be no successful race to the top if we all use different types of roads and vehicles to get there. *Expectations* are critical to set a course of action while *targets* and *tools* provide data and management solutions for leaders. The roads and vehicles must be standardized for education commerce to flow and a transparent educational market driven economy to serve the public good. Common infrastructure is so simple to understand in other industries, yet when we talk infrastructure in high schools, it is like my dad used to say: "Talking to you is like talking to the wall."

I know that using an analogy has limitations. This particular analogy is necessary because my experience tells me that the concept of infrastructure is a tough sell in education. Instead of standardization of roads and vehicles educators often want to talk about wild ideas like jet packs, unicycles, duck boats, and off-road vehicles. Like any other profession, innovators run the gamut from genius inventors to flat-out crazy high school teachers. The difference is we have a history of these folks being left alone to invent vehicles to transport our kids to worlds unknown. I am amazed that we often don't have a clear picture of our destination or our route. Thus, I ask you to take a deep breath and read this chapter with great care.

So what is infrastructure in education? It is no different from infrastructure for travel and commerce. The *expectation shift* describes what types of destinations we will build (like city centers, suburbs, rural communities). The *target shift* is the pathways we will travel from one destination to another (the roads). The *tools shift* is the means we will use to travel (cars, SUVs, buses, trucks). Think about the courage of political and business leaders to build our national highway system. Did the farmer in Plymouth, Indiana, understand this work? Probably not. However, without this work, he could not have expanded his operation to sell his crops to consumers and factories around the world.

Other countries are ahead of the U.S. on educational infrastructure. They have common standards, they have common learning systems, they have common metrics, and they can communicate well and move goods and services seamlessly. I would argue that our slip in math performance in the world standings is mostly due to our lack of learning infrastructure. Farmers in Indiana can out-perform farmers in the third world due to the U.S. infrastructure (and standardization in the technology and tools for farming in the U.S.). I stay up at night knowing that our focus on using education as a political instrument with state and local control will stand in the way of building the real infrastructure that we need to accelerate learning and innovation in high schools.

### *Expectations: The Expectations Shift*

At the turn of the century, Gary, Indiana, just a few miles north of Crown Point, was at the heart of the industrial revolution, producing steel to build a new world. The idea that all organizations could be tailor-made for efficiency and productivity based on an industrial manufacturing model caught on like wildfire in the educational community. Schools were built to model factories. Through this worldview, workers (students) were compliant and happy Dr. Seuss-like characters; they moved when they heard bells, did their prescribed tasks (homework), and nobody had to think too much to have a happy life in "School-ville." Through the heart of the prosperous industrial age there were well paying, low-skilled jobs for the vast number of high school dropouts that our "efficient system" threw off like scrap metal.

The sheer force and muscle of the American industrial machine lead the U.S. through two world wars. The post World War II baby boom *Happy Days* economy created a false sense of effectiveness of the industrial model in industry and education. In the middle of the twentieth century, a quality movement emerged that shaped a new world marketplace. The quality movement simply challenged all members of organizations to embrace teamwork and accountability—shared leadership for results. Giants of American industry initially ignored the movement, while post-war Japanese industrial leaders took cutting edge theories of quality management and moved from cheap and shoddy products to the one of the world leaders in manufacturing and production.

American industry faced a choice: retool or die. The American public high school was not challenged in the new world marketplace because there was no real global competition. Thus, the "scrap metal" most public high schools continue to produce from their industrial origins now creates insurmountable barriers for growth and innovation. The expectations have shifted, and schools are challenged to do something that they have never done before—prepare all students for a new global economy. The "scrap metal" that continues to be thrown off today will not find employment in the rapidly changing American global economic engine that now requires higher skilled, twenty-first century workers.

In its defense, the American public high school was never designed to help all students succeed in post secondary education, training, careers, and life. The American public high school was built to sort! Sorting was an appropriate function when there were good paying jobs for high school dropouts. Most high schools, quite simply, produce the results they were designed to produce. The great sorting engine we call "the industrial age public high school" generally cranked out one-third for college, one-third for middle management, and one-third for low-skilled factory jobs. The sorting machine served this country well through the industrial age. The sorting machine will no longer serve America in a new global economy.

Fundamentally, the expectations have shifted over the last few decades. The American public high school has to retool and embrace the quality management movement that began over fifty years ago that has demonstrated results in current successful U.S. industries. There can be no hesitation, as the American public high school must increase its efficiency and productivity to reclaim a position of excellence and relevance in the new global economy.

We are challenged to define what twenty-first century high schools look like. How do these schools help all students build an individual plan for success? How do we retool the personnel and support systems to ensure that every student is successful beyond high school? What does a great urban, suburban, and rural high school that prepares all kids for post-secondary success look like? These environments will look as different as towns, suburbs, and cities, but they will serve their citizens based on a common set of clearly defined national and international college and workforce readiness outcomes. A common national high school transcript will help schools understand the expectations and build their communities (schools) to best serve their citizens (students).

### Targets: From state standards to college and workforce readiness

The United States was originally not so united when the thirteen colonies took on and defeated the powerful British Army to secure our independence. We now have a fifty-headed monster that has no chance against determined emerging superpowers like China and India who have more honor students than we have students. As all states are responsible for educating their citizenry, each state has spent millions of dollars reinventing the wheel by inviting educators to the state capital and asking them what students should know and

---

**! SOLUTIONS**

The common high school transcript is the vital first step in establishing the groundwork for infrastructure. This is not complicated. The national transcript will have simple, established metrics and information that is the "baseline" for college and career success. There are common and agreed upon information like ACT, SAT, Advanced Placement, Work Keys, Common Courses, that are standardized and internationally benchmarked.

Infrastructure should start with a clear definition of what we are to produce in our schools.

Yes I know what is coming next—the claws are out on the educating the whole child folks. I am one of those folks as well. If you read the beginning of the book on how we created a value system at the high school to promote and drive powerful living portraits of our graduates, you should realize I am on your side.

Here is my point—we do not have infrastructure to help us look at student performance to then act to accelerate college and workforce readiness. A common set of national metrics is critical for this purpose. My purpose for this book is to help folks understand that eating an elephant starts with the first few bites. These first bites are clearly focused on standardization in measurement.

do. Some states may have been sharp enough to invite a business professional or college professor to join the conversation. But the results are similar: in a highly scripted process akin to a large and colorful bird mating ritual, we roll out our proud state standards for public comment. The public generally has no comment, mesmerized by the primal bird contortions as the governor, state superintendent, and chamber of commerce all applaud the newly revised state standards.

Fortunately there is a new conversation in the country that brings to bear deep empirical research on college and workforce readiness. National groups like ACT, Achieve, and College Board have brought their research to the table to help drive a new set of common national standards for college and workforce readiness. Let's examine ACT, the college testing company. ACT has tracked successful students though college. Then they worked backwards to identify what these students learned in high school to help them succeed to build a set of college readiness standards. I know that this makes too much sense for education, but thank goodness groups are doing more things that make more sense. Moreover, ACT and other groups have developed instruments beginning in middle school through the college transition to help students and schools more thoughtfully plan for success.

Along with emerging national college and workforce readiness standards, a twenty-first century skills movement is sweeping across the country. How do our students find relevant information in an information society? How do our students communicate ideas clearly and powerfully in team settings? Industry leaders have been advocates for a long time. This is not a new conversation. The problem has always been "how do we measure" twenty-first century skills to meet the needs of a new twenty-first century learner and worker. There are now instruments from ACT and other organizations to assess behaviors like teamwork, persistence, and organization beginning in middle school. The ability to measure these skills will drive a new set of outcomes for college and career readiness due to students demonstrating more effective workplace behaviors in their first real job (being a good high school student).

College and workforce readiness and twenty-first century skills are the new targets all schools must embrace to provide students the best competitive edge in the new global economy. High schools that rally teams of teachers, administrators, students, and parents around this information to make decisions and drive improvements are beginning the process of retooling toward a new nationally defined standard of excellence.

If we again return to our analogy, we need to drive on the right roads. We have some current, internationally benchmarked roads that lead us to college and workplace success. We are using these roads in variable ways and not everyone on the road knows where they are going or how fast to travel. Parents sign up for the ACT or SAT, departments of workforce development administer the ACT Work Keys, teachers give A.P. tests, and yet all this information is not accessible to everyone in the system. The

## ! SOLUTIONS

The grand mistake we often make in education is to work on defining standards when we have no information about current reality. The second step after the common transcript is to actually use the strong existing instruments we have to assess the college and workforce readiness of our students more broadly.

Groups are doing good work developing the common core national standards, but for high schools, we have internationally benchmarked instruments like the ACT and Advanced Placement.

Measure the skills of our students more broadly and provide the information to students, parents, teachers, administrators, business leaders, and politicians to help guide decisions. The second bite of the elephant is measuring college and workforce readiness with the best existing tools we have while stronger standards and instruments are developed.

roadmaps have to be charted and provided for everyone, and this is possible after we have a common national transcript. GPS systems need to be developed and placed in the hands of every student, parent, teacher, and administrator.

### *Tools: From technology as optional to technology as central*

I was talking to a teacher about her laptop. She loved the access and tools and then talked about her kids not needing this experience. "They need me, the text book, and intense face to face work in classrooms." Huh? I asked her if we needed more real contact instead of sending information to her via email and would she kindly turn in her laptop and grab an old grade book out of storage. She declined with a strange look on her face, and at first walked slowly away, then sped up as she passed the guidance office. We routinely see and hear teachers using twenty-first century tools for adult work, but when they cross the classroom door, it's like some portal that takes them back in time to drive old practices for student work.

What will students encounter as they enter the twenty-first century work-place? Let's see, the tools of the twenty-first century work place? Land a knowledge job, receive a laptop, and get to work on the first day. Step 1: open the lid. Step 2: type www.google.com. Step 3: enter the professional stream like a salmon running to the ocean. Twenty-first century professional work is simple—work as a team, find relevant information, develop solutions, make the enterprise successful and profitable.

Okay, so we are still riding bicycles in many of our high school classrooms. We know we need a vehicle to help everyone in the system drive hard on the right roads to the clearly established destinations. We know we need that GPS system in the hands of the real drivers, the students.

What is holding high schools back? Let's examine an example to better illustrate this issue. Why did teenagers in Mexico all have mobile phones before teens in the richest country in the world? When there are not well established industries, there are no barriers for innovation and growth. There were no landline phone company monopolies that blocked innovation in Mexico. Thus, mobile technologies leaped ahead to serve Mexico stronger and quicker than the United States. From this example we can make the leap to consider the position of the influential American textbook industry.

We can't allow textbook companies to drive eighteenth century work in a twenty-first century economy. In case you have not noticed, content is free online. What is more, the free content is from the great libraries and universities around the world. There are lectures, simulations, primary source documents that have defined the history of mankind, and I can go on and on. I call this phenomenon the "bottled water" issue for high schools. We don't have money to waste paying for bottled water anymore. We have to place tools in the hands of our students and teach them how to fish for good information. The money we are spending on textbooks creates a tremendous barrier to develop infrastructure that serves the needs of the twenty-first century learner.

The textbook industry should be in the same situation as the newspaper industry with providing free content online. Due to political influence and the lack of a real free market in education, we continue to subsidize

## ! SOLUTIONS

How do we make decisions in education? We need to make decisions based on research and learning in the service of kids and communities. Recall my nuclear engineering friend who left the profession out of frustration. The right placement for the nuclear reactor was not where it was actually built.

Textbooks are not the answer in a twenty-first century workplace. After 1995 I have not worked in an environment that has widely used books and nor should our students.

the textbook industry business model and sacrifice the money that could be invested in infrastructure development to purchase bottled water when there is perfectly good tap water online. Millions of dollars in perpetual yearly lease payments to the textbook companies could be spent on better resources to support student learning and growth.

### ❗ SOLUTIONS

There is clearly a need to think about redirecting the money that is spent on textbooks to tools. There are three simple needs for the vehicles to work:

→ All high schools must be wireless environments.

→ All students must have a learning appliance in their hands (computer, tablet, smartphone, etc.).

→ All schools need to use a common learning system to share good free packaged content so assessment data can flow to all stakeholders.

The smartest schools are grabbing free content and packaging it for student consumption. Every original historical document in the world is available online for free. The smartest schools are designing activities like international debates using tools like the online videoconferencing application Skype. The smartest schools are helping their students solve real problems like clean water and hunger through research and social networking to raise awareness and money.

A last note for the cranky adults who continue to say, "those darn kids." Why do we fight the technology tools of the twenty-first century in high schools? It is a bizarre world in education where we talk way too much about policing iPods and iPads, tracking texted pictures of students with Cheetos in their nose, and closing off access to the flatulence version of the "Sweet Home Alabama" on YouTube. These are the tools that are in the hands of students. These are also the tools that are in the hands of professionals. It is our responsibility as the authors of twenty-first century education to work in partnership with our students, parents, and communities to teach the appropriate, ethical, and effective use of these tools. We must embrace this responsibility as we also build cars that go over 100 miles per hour and throw our teenagers the keys! The right vehicles for learning are necessary. Teaching responsibility to use these vehicles is equally necessary.

# CHAPTER FOUR

*"Processes don't do work, people do."*

JOHN SEELY BROWN

Education is a people business. The educational space is filled with caring and compassionate folks who want the best for kids. Oftentimes, these caring and compassionate people don't work very well in our deficit model of planning. We beat them up, label them as failures, and expect them to go the extra mile. In order to develop talent, I advocate that we recognize and build on the good things we do for kids—drive more good things and systematically bring in the training for the gaps that need to be addressed.

Let me provide an example. Our education system is in a constant debate around the role of testing. I have a very simple way of thinking about this work that is not deficit thinking. I will assume for a moment that we agree that the test we will use here is an appropriate measure of student knowledge and skills. Teaching to the test is an appropriate step towards teaching skills to meet standards. We all move through a progression of understanding expectations and checking to see if we hit them.

The beginning of this process looks pretty mechanical, as you might expect. For most strong teachers I have observed, step one is to review the test questions like the ACT or an Advanced Placement test. This process helps the

> **! SOLUTIONS**
>
> Teaching to the test is not a bad thing. It is a necessary first step in helping students perform on a new set of expectations. The key is that the test is a strong measure of a student actually demonstrating the necessary skills. Tests like the ACT and Advanced Placement provide good data back to teachers to help them understand how their students performed. These are great tools that need to be embraced, and the data needs to flow into state data systems to flow seamlessly back to teachers. The infrastructure for data sharing is critical in this process.

> **! SOLUTIONS**
>
> Japanese companies embraced this teamwork for accountability to dramatically improve manufacturing (as mentioned in the Expectations Shift). These same skills are applied to student outcomes when teachers collaborate around data, training, and sharing instructional practices.

teacher to understand the content, depth, and form. These are all important aspects of student performance that teachers need to know and understand. As the teacher begins to receive data on student performance, they begin to see the connection to standards. The next progression I often witness is teachers then work with a team of professionals to receive training on effective practice. Additionally, in the best professional environments, teachers also receive training on how to be a strong professional team to managing better results for kids. This is a fun and powerful process and transition in the life cycle of a high school teacher. To move through this progression, high school teachers need some time and training. We also have to expect that teacher and student growth is not a straight line. As teachers learn new concepts and improve, we have to respect that failure is a part of growing. Thus, to build on strengths we have to set high expectations for teachers that respect a real growth process that has room for failure and learning in a team setting. This process is the most important micro function of high schools in preparing more students for college and career success. Talented principals, administrators, and teacher leaders are doing this type of work in high schools with the best data they can gather.

### *Training: From teacher as worker to student as worker*

Educator Phil Schletcty was talking at a conference back in 1994. He talked about what Martians would say if they came down to earth and observed a traditional American high school. "It is a place where a bunch of young people come to watch a few old people work." If this is the case, then we have a problem.

To be clear, I am not advocating that teachers do not need to present information well and take time in a whole group setting to do activities. I am advocating that the best learning environments look like the best work environments. The best managers, teachers, and coaches get results from groups of people individually and collectively. There is no one-way to do this. However, we know when we are on a team with a good coach or manager driving us individually and collectively toward results.

As we look back on our best mentors, coaches, managers, and teachers, they all have a few simple things in common:

1. They made us feel valued and knew what made us tick like a psychologist.
2. They sold us on the task like a salesman.
3. They knew their stuff; they were experts.
4. They used a variety of techniques for teaching and guiding the work like the best practitioners.
5. They held us accountable for our personal best, just as a mentor would.
6. They held the team accountable for collective results like a coach.
7. They built a sense of community in the classroom as a leader.

## ❗ SOLUTIONS

The solution for developing teachers to drive self-directed twenty-first century learners can be found in our highest performing elementary schools. There you will find grade level teams looking at good data from reading and basic math assessments. You will find consistency in student work experiences based on what is producing results. You will find caring adults that hold each other accountable and responsible for results.

The lack of infrastructure in the high school is a huge barrier in allowing teachers to use data to develop strong team solutions for kids. Thus, you find pockets of isolated innovation where we "kind of know" it is working well based on some data, professional judgment, and student and parent feedback.

I have a hunch that university professors really do understand learning and try very hard to equip bright young teacher candidates with a powerful toolkit. The issue is that these teachers walk into an environment of very little data for teachers to receive feedback. Thus, historically, average teaching and learning behaviors go unchallenged and the status quo continues. Young idealistic high school teachers conform to the reality around them.

IBM spent millions of dollars in the 1980s researching learning to conclude that learning is a negotiation of mutual relevance. The best teachers design the best negotiations that have powerful relevance where students engage fully in the task with commitment and produce big results. Negotiations don't have to be complicated or over-engineered. Negotiations happen between teachers and students, students and students, students and materials; this could be as simple as a good book. Negotiations happen between students and tutors, students and technology; this could mean computer games, research, and practice.

As a parent, what does your student talk about at the dinner table that inspires them to work hard in class? What are the work products that your student has taken the most time, commitment, and pride in producing? There you will find your student functioning as a twenty-first century worker! There you will find a powerhouse twenty-first century teacher.

### *Relationships: From By Chance to By Design*

When you see a Hollywood movie star do public service announcements on education, it is clear that some teacher made a difference in his or her life. Powerful relationships happen routinely in high schools across the country. The only problem is most high schools operate in a model of relationship by chance. The classic American high school is a smorgasbord of hundreds of courses. Kids are run through courses throughout the day; some connect with teachers, and some don't. Some students are fortunate to play sports or get involved with clubs where they connect with an adult, but too many don't.

What kind of dining experience do people have at smorgasbords? Wasting food, waiting until the hot stuff comes out, cutting in line, being messy and rude, not tipping well—ouch! These seem to be the behaviors that many frustrated high school teachers and administrators often complain about: Oh those darn kids.

This is not really an educational problem so to speak. It has more to do with sociology. How do we better group people with common interests, goals, and talents to maximize the opportunity for relationships to develop that will lead to a lasting impact on the lives of the students we serve? Or in other words, how do we move from relationships by chance to relationships by design?

There are two researched strategies that create the conditions to place students in a focused, fine dining experience and out of the smorgasbord. When dining well, I seldom see an individual without a napkin in their lap.

### *Student Identity: Program-Based Learning Communities*

There are many ways to organize to support the needs of students, but the college research on smaller learning communities is glaringly clear. Most universities group students in a variety of ways to ensure their successful completion. Students first define an identity—say, electrical engineering. Then students of like identity are grouped together to develop a small supportive learning community. What "academic identity" or "academic label" do most high school students possess?

### *Adult-Student Relationships: Program-Based Advisors*

There must be an adult in the learning community who feels a great sense of responsibility for the success of each individual student. Given a student-to-counselor ratio in many high schools of over 400-to-one or more, it won't be the counselor. Most high schools have instituted a student resource time, and most successful high schools implement rigorous social, academic, and individual mental health programming for all students within the context of the student resource time. Each student is assigned an adult mentor based on shared interests. Learning from the research and results from universities, that mentor has the same academic identity as the student—electrical engineering faculty with electrical engineering students. Part-

**! SOLUTIONS**

The strategies provided in the text have one major requirement. Students through their middle school years need to be challenged and exposed to careers and opportunities. These real-world experiences will help students and families set career goals. In the American culture, where everyone has a chance to be a doctor, we have to be careful with how this is positioned. This is not a life decision. This is a process of being more thoughtful about planning for the future. This is an opportunity to create relevance in programs and relationships with caring adults.

nering students and faculty based on program identity and interests maximizes the authenticity of the relationship and provides a potential mentor for life.

To be clear, students in high schools are not being tracked here. They are being challenged to set goals and enter a community with shared goals. If and when students change goals, they enter a new community.

### Leadership: From the Great Man to a Community of Leaders

The most obvious example of the American public high school retaining its industrial origins is the role of the high school principal. The public often looks at one person as the great or not-so-great man or woman in the main office. American companies that held on to their industrial leadership origins of a great man in the office making all the decisions during the quality management movement, quite simply, died. It became labor versus management, and everyone lost.

A few years ago I was sitting on a plane next to a union labor attorney and consultant. He said something that I will never forget. He said that they are not invited into companies and factories that have established a shared leadership vision and plan. When true leadership is present, everyone has representation. The only time when representation is truly needed is when there is a lack of leadership.

Japanese organizations led the total quality movement by empowering everyone in the organization to be leaders and problem solvers focused intensely on the quality of the product. Great organizations don't have heroic leaders; they have leaders at every level and position who serve the mission of the organization and make sure that people are in the right positions to maximize their talents. Leadership emerges from within the organization when it is needed from the right people and groups. This is simply called leadership capacity. The solution here is a checklist of components to drive leadership capacity and ensure quality and results.

***Community Agreements:*** In order to create an environment of learning, growth, and continuous improvement, people need to feel safe taking risks. Since this is not a natural instinct for people who have not worked in environments that cultivate risk, a set of clear agreements must be developed across the community that values this new cultural expectation. If one person or group in the organization violates the trust and community agreements, it is not the leader, but leadership—courageous individuals—from within the organization that protects the risk-taking environment to allow for leadership to spread throughout the community.

## ! SOLUTIONS

I literally list every stakeholder in the school. Underneath each group I list the communication strategies I use to make sure our message is clearly communicated. I also have weekly communication meetings to discuss what information is shared. I walk around the building and consistently ask my faculty leadership reps what information folks need. I consistently ask my administrative team who needs to know what. Communication is tough, and there is no one way to do it. Get out and talk to people to find out what they need!

***Explicit Beliefs:*** What will you resign over? Leadership capacity can't develop unless there is a clear and explicit guiding force that drives the work of leaders; many call this moral purpose. All students have unique gifts, all students can succeed, all students need a caring adult in their life at the school, etc. The school must take time to clearly define these beliefs.

***Clear Roles, Responsibilities, and A Plan of Action for all Leadership Groups:*** Great families assign chores. The best families post those chores around the house, and all the members of the family hold one another accountable for results. Leaders of the organization must place the right people in the right seats and must remove those people who can't produce or who violate the community agreements. These are often the same folks.

***Communication Plan (Marketing 101):*** The flow of information is critical in large organizations. Multiple strategies must be implemented to ensure individuals are informed and contribute to the mission. Communication must be perceived as supportive.

***Celebrations and Rituals:*** Leadership emerges when organizations celebrate successes together. I believe that as former coaches and teachers, many high school leaders understand this chapter the best. We know how to mobilize and energize people. We know what good teaching and learning looks like. We know how to talk with individuals to understand their needs. These skills will be maximized to support student success when the infrastructure, partnerships, and innovation shifts take place.

**SOLUTIONS**

I know that many great leaders do this really well. I will share one really simple strategy that I use in a big school. Each month we have a short faculty meeting. I set out spirit cards on the tables and ask everyone to write a note to a colleague based on a prompt I give them like, "Who shares the most valuable information and strategies to help support you as a professional and provide an example." I collect those cards and read them because it makes me feel good. Then I walk around the building during the day and hand the cards to the deserving teachers during their class. I want the teachers to be excited when the principal walks in the room.

# CHAPTER FIVE

*"Geography has made us neighbors. History has made us friends. Economics has made us partners, and necessity has made us allies."*

JOHN F. KENNEDY

Partnership is an overused word in education. There are tons of relationships and very few partnerships. Partnerships are special relationships where both parties have an interest, worked on the planning, and are recipients of value produced by the partnership. High school buildings are often the central hub of the community for many things that often include a ball and or a field. In fact, athletics can be an extremely healthy part of the fabric of a community and can be a model for what an effective partnership looks like. The more difficult challenge is to form partnerships that impact the work that is done in schools between the hours of 8 a.m. and 3 p.m.

Partnerships are about acting locally and regionally. The leaders of the local and regional organizations are committed to high school communities. They advertise in our athletic programs, their children compete on our fields, and their grandchildren are admitted to good colleges after we serve them well. Oftentimes, they are the "over-served" and don't see the urgency for change because they have been successful in the current system. They were the upper third of the great sorting machine, and when you are sorted to the top you have a hard time relating to the issues experienced by the groups that are sorted elsewhere.

I recognize that there are many examples of schools that have developed strong partnerships with business, parents, community agencies, universities, and trade organizations. The point of this chapter is to provide a clear vision so that more schools can develop the meaningful relationships with stakeholders, and to move those relationships into partnerships that support the post-secondary success of all students. I have separated parents from other partnerships because parents play a special role in the success of high school students.

### *Parents: From Parent Observers to Parent Participants*

There is one place on the planet where there is consistently no achievement gap by race, ethnicity, gender, or economic status. The U.S. military schools have cracked the code to drive equity in outcomes for kids. U.S. military schools have created an environment that powerfully engages parents. It is amazing that we don't hear more about these special learning institutions. If there were a magic bullet in public education, I would place my money on the parents. Parents who set high expectations, model behaviors, and hold students accountable are invaluable in our high school equation.

U.S. military schools do have the advantage, given that the parents are employed by the U.S. military. Military schools deserve credit for setting clear expectations for families as partners to keep kids on the right track and moving forward. If any problems arise, a call from the commander is just what the principal ordered. Immediate results!

The power of the fully engaged parent is not a mystery or new revelation. The question has always been how do public schools create the same set of expectations and develop the right kind of programs, tools, and leverage to engage all parents? Traditionally, when students come to public high schools, parents often disengage because they can't seem to find a place to plug in. Kids naturally give their folks the classic, "Aw, Mom. Come on." High school kids are searching for identity in social peer groups, and they think that parents cramp their style.

This is actually the most critical time where students need supervision and strong adult mentoring in their lives. This is where high schools and parents have often not been able to effectively connect. The front doors are locked, the classes have titles like honors chemistry, and there appears to be little opportunity to really contribute other than fundraising in athletics, which is not all that inspiring for most parents.

First, what do successful parents do currently? Parents of the most successful kids have found a way to keep connected. They supervise their kids, they communicate with counselors and teachers, they help their students focus on their future, and they do the research to best position their children for success. The most successful parents think of themselves as educational brokers and have these brokering skills.

## SOLUTIONS

For schools, what three simple strategies translate into results for kids? Based on our data, we have found three measurable parent strategies that produce results for kids. Parents could sign a simple compact with the school to ensure these three strategies are implemented for all kids.

It is a simple career skill to make sure your child gets to school on time and attends every day.

You don't have to know honors chemistry, but you can talk to your child each week and look at grades online nowadays. If your child's grades are not what you expect, reach out and contact a teacher or counselor and set up a meeting. The biggest thing is to follow through on meetings and strategies, and have a follow up checkpoint to celebrate improvement.

There is abundant data promoting the benefits of extracurricular participation for many reasons. Make sure your child is engaged in and completes an extracurricular activity at school. They are positive adult-sponsored peer groups.

Here is a letter I received from a parent.

*Dr. Ban,*

*I am Lauren Cain's mom, and I am sending this e-mail to thank you for the wonderful opportunities that Lauren had at CPHS. I know that Lauren e-mailed you to tell you about her credit status from her AP tests and how thrilled we were. We just received more information from the University of Indianapolis—because of Lauren's dual credit chemistry class they are giving her another eight credits towards her degree, which means she is starting her freshman year with a total of twenty-eight credits. These credits equal a year of college with tuition being $22,000 a year at U Indy.*

*If you have any parent meetings for underclassmen parents, I would be more than happy to sit on a panel or help in way possible to talk about the real impact of what you offer and how people really need to take advantage of all of the opportunities at CPHS.*

*Kathy Cain, Parent*

What schools need to do is to arm parents who have not developed these brokering skills with materials that help them cut through the red tape and navigate a confusing system. (By the way, most schools don't see themselves as big, intimidating, and confusing). The best schools are becoming more oriented toward customer service and provide parents with a simple and usable set of tools they need to help their adolescent succeed.

Additionally, schools must harness the power of parent leaders to help other parents. When I first arrived at Crown Point we had a Bridge Builders parent group that convened at the school once a month. A small group of parents really enjoyed this activity because they wanted information. As we moved grades online, rebuilt the website, which is updated daily, sent weekly automated parent phone calls, and email monthly departmental updates, the "receiving information" function of Bridge Builders became unnecessary. A few leadership parents had the courage to step up and construct a new parent organization called parent ambassadors. These leadership parents have embraced the vision of parents helping parents. They organize freshman parent orientations, how to schedule your student nights, parent Advanced Placement night, navigating college admissions night, and many more. They are a force in our community, and I am humbled to work with them. The next vision we have is that every parent ambassador will be trained on college planning to provide a huge cadre of well-informed parent resources that are available for all parents to have help managing the college admissions and scholarship game.

## Partnerships: From Isolationism to Strategic Partnerships

The *Titanic* sailed alone—enough said.

> **! SOLUTIONS**
>
> Parents are a huge part of the student success equation. As infrastructure is developed at the national, state, and local levels, parents have access to information and tools like never before to become that educational broker for their child.
>
> We always talk about the move from bank tellers to online banking at Crown Point. We don't need more tellers in the school. We need infrastructure so that information flows in clear and manageable ways to our customers.
>
> Our parent leaders are working hard on developing the online college planning tools to help all parents manage the post-secondary trajectories and plans with their students.

High schools must turn to natural partners of higher learning, workforce development, parents, and community agencies to support the success of all students in cultures of continuous improvement. I believe that most people understand the intense economic conditions that will now require us to innovate and align work across community organizations to support one another.

How difficult is the joint venture, the merger? What type of leadership is required to partner in education, the most regulated industry in American society? Is it possible to really connect at the core beliefs of these institutions and break through the industrial baggage, bureaucracy, regulatory challenges, and bad behavior of shortsighted people? This shift is, quite honestly, the toughest. Why? We have worked in silos for so long we really don't know where or how to begin a merger. There are many examples of powerful school community partnerships. Most examples are based on the talent of a person or group that inspires and creates commitments and value for both partners. Oftentimes, when the individual or group moves on or loses interest, the partnership falls apart. Thus, we have some wonderful individuals that inspire commitment, build models, and produce results. Once again, the lack of infrastructure provides barriers for partnerships to become sustainable. Most often the data is on someone's computer in an Excel spreadsheet. If that person is hit by a bus, goodbye partnership!

The American public high school must once again become the hub of the community. Not only should the high school host athletic and music competitions and performances, it should hum as the initial economic and social engine of the community. It must construct learning partnerships with parents and community agencies to support all students. Most of all, it should partner with colleges, trade schools, and workforce development to create a more relevant and valuable community hub.

There are four clear partnership initiatives that need to take place in the American

## (RR) REFLECTION

The New American Research High School site plays an important regional leadership role. Plans and models have to be constructed for high schools to participate in partnership work. Data has to be collected and evaluated for effectiveness.

Example: This site will provide for one clear owner of the plan, process, and management structure for dual credit. The infrastructure concept keeps surfacing as a regional university would like to have one model, one major contact point to high schools and one smaller and focused work team to help make ongoing decisions to improve the model for the region.

The regional university simply cannot manage sixteen school district relationships in one county very well. There has to be a partnership structure and plan.

public high school. Each of these initiatives requires strong planning and talented people for full realization. Most schools do not have the internal skill sets or capacity to realize these partnerships. I would advocate that the New American Research High School take the lead role in establishing the regional partnership models to export to a regional network of high schools. The partnership models for the following three initiatives should be developed at a regional research high school site.

* Develop partnerships with social service agencies to provide families and students support.

* Develop partnerships with trade schools and colleges to offer degree credit and certifications.

* Develop partnerships with local business to provide structured work and learning environments for students.

Economic conditions and higher expectations will challenge high schools to partner in order to survive.

# CHAPTER SIX

*"Every organization must be prepared to abandon
everything it does to survive in the future."*

PETER DRUCKER

Driving innovation addresses fundamental beliefs that are often buried under the pervasive management work of most American public high schools. When I was in the private sector, my whole world was innovation for an entire year. I remember practitioners coming to Dallas who were so envious that I was able to do that work. They were the ones that pointed out that they were able to maybe carve out a small sliver of their time and energy to work on innovation. Innovation, invention, research, and development are powerful words in business, medicine, engineering, and the other major fields in a global economy. Russia's dramatic budget cut of science and technology research and development over the last ten years has placed this former Space Race competitor a generation behind. When was the last time your read a spy novel where Russia and the U.S. were locked in a race to invent?

In every industry in the world, the research and development budget is a sacred cow. Try to touch Google's or Microsoft's R&D budget—not on your life. Where is the clear and explicit R&D focus in education? The idea of R&D in high school is the foundation for the last section of this book. Research and development has to be as high a priority in education as it is in medicine. If I said to you, let's go to the Mayo Clinic, the University of Chicago hospital, or the Houston Medical Center, immediately you would know that these are institutions where cutting edge practices are developed, tested, and shared with the world.

Research in high schools most often emerges from the investment in a reform agenda in urban centers. For example, Chicago, Boston, Houston, Los Angeles, New York all see investment and have well-established university partners. Much of this work is productive and helps inform our practice. The lack of infrastructure once again creates barriers for these practices to be transferred effectively.

I would argue that the lack of infrastructure (specifically the standardization of outcomes) raises questions about the effectiveness of these reform initiatives altogether. I also question the connection that these reforms have with economic development. Finally, many of the reforms and innovations from the urban centers don't necessarily translate well to different high school settings like suburbia and rural America. If the U.S. is committed to establishing the best system to launch fourteen to eighteen-year-olds into a competitive and productive future, then Americans must recognize and advocate for research and development in a variety of high school settings linked to regional economic development. If the current economic data and unemployment rate does not create a sense of urgency and the need to commit research dollars to community as well as school reform, than we have truly lost a critical opportunity for educational reform. If the U.S. is committed to maintaining research universities, inventing new markets and products, and igniting a fire in our economy to create a better standard of living for more families, then investing in top performing high schools and challenging them to move from high-performing to ground breaking should be a top priority.

### *Research: From "I Feel" to "The Research Says"*

In a recent all-day workshop, a team of math teachers evaluated math textbooks and materials from a variety of sources. A team of experts guided them from the Dana Center at the University of Texas. The evaluation process was designed to find the materials that scored highest according to strong research-based evaluation tools. The teachers were a bit surprised that a non-traditional set of materials scored highest. When asked which set of materials they would most likely select, they chose, in unison, the materials that received the lowest score.

If this were an exercise in health care, a team of doctors would be held accountable and sued for malpractice. Yet in education, many decisions are made from a lens of adult preference, emotion or comfort. To be frank, the field of education is made up of kind and passionate people who often work on emotion rather than data and research. There is no question that "people work" requires flexibility, compassion, and an emotional intelligence. However, the future of education should be guided by what is proven to work for kids.

The gap of research and practice has been wide as the Grand Canyon in education. The fact that innovation spreads so slowly in education is one issue, but the real issue is the expectation of the high school teacher. As teachers, we have been asked to do too many things that are not expectations in other professions. Let's take a family physician as an example. As a professional, our family physicians are practitioners who implement research-based practices that have proven to show results in clinical trials. They don't claim to

## ! SOLUTIONS

We expect too much from teachers, and then beat them up when they don't produce. In business, we call this scope creep. Teachers are mostly nice individuals who have allowed people to expand their job description.

Let's simplify the teacher role:

+ Know your content.
+ Know the best instructional methods.
+ Know how to connect with kids.
+ Know how to manage groups of kids.
+ Know how to collaborate with adults.
+ Be trainable.
+ Work hard.
+ Communicate well.
+ Be positive.

Lets take the following off the plate:

+ Research best practice like a maniac.
+ Invent new practices daily.
+ Tap dance.

If you expect teachers to invent and research, they need to be trained and be provided the time to do this work. Teachers in the research high school (in a real R&D setting) will be expected to invent new practice, but this is a special breed of teacher, just as research faculty in hospitals are a special breed.

be inventors. Our best family physicians are part of a team of physicians who are trained to implement healthcare programs and build strong, trusting relationships with patients. In education, though, our teachers are challenged to be researchers, inventors, and practitioners. In fact, you can find thousands of professional journal articles on teachers as researchers. We don't ask physicians to go into their labs and mix up remedies to test on patients, yet this explicitly happens every day in schools across the country. How effective do you think most teachers are at mixing up the chemicals for student success in the boiler rooms of public high schools?

Our best teachers are the ones who have been prepared and have received embedded and on-going professional development in school-based teams on programs and practices that have a clear track record of success. They implement these programs with fidelity and build powerful relationships with kids and families. Our best teachers are very similar to our best physicians insofar as they're professional practitioners. As educators, we have to stop being sold by textbook salesmen who claim the textbook, workbook, support materials that go boom, and a free LCD projector is going to make a difference in learning for kids. We have to look for well-proven programming and instruction to better serve our kids and communities.

### *Innovation in Education Spreading Like Wildfire*

It is no surprise that high schools are slow to adopt new ideas. The industrial baggage that we retain from our initial design as a learning factory lends itself to teachers working in isolation. In most professional settings in the world, the professionals work together in teams towards goals. In most American high schools, teachers spend most of their day with kids, isolated from other professionals.

In Japan, many teachers spend half of their day in intense professional dialog and planning. Their belief is that through this process of professional discussion and debate, powerful ideas will surface for the benefit of all kids, and they will produce better results. The factory design of the American high school programs teachers to stay in their place on the factory floor, their classroom. American learning structures often stand in the way of teachers to be able to learn together and innovate. Isn't it interesting how recent industrial innovation has not heavily influenced education? Are we willing to pay the price for the changes needed? Note the comparison below.

|  | **American** | **Japanese** |
| --- | --- | --- |
| **Industrial Origin** | *Leaders in the Industrial Revolution* | *Leaders in Total Quality Management* |
|  | *Managers Define Processes* | *Teamwork = Results* |
| **Educational Reality** | *High Schools reflect a factory design and teachers often work in isolation in their rooms.* | *High schools reflect a team orientation with shared professional space and time.* |

It is tough to know when you take down mammoths in high schools. The big goal is to identify this through common assessments on a common learning system. If teachers are using the same assessments and the same learning platform across the state, we can begin to see mammoths go down through the whole state with a click of a button. This is *way* better than cave drawings!

Through the history of mankind, humans have learned and innovated on the job in groups. This is why there is very little innovation in traditional American public high schools. Humans are social learning animals. The woolly mammoth hunt began for a group of brave hunters. One hunter replayed a carefully designed move in his mind and approached the mammoth with his spear. He leaped and released the spear with lethal accuracy and precision, providing the tribe with food, clothing, and tools. The hunting move that produced results was not only celebrated, it was modeled throughout the tribe. The elders carefully painted the move on walls and told the story of the hunt that would be passed down for generations. Every hunter practiced the move. Every boy in the tribe emulated the move with any stick he could find. Prehistoric man had the infrastructure he needed to innovate. He clearly knew he produced results as the mammoth was taken down and the entire tribe was fed and clothed. These results were clear, transparent, and public. He had the technology he needed to accomplish his task, and the tribe had the communication channels to spread the innovation throughout the tribe so everyone could produce the same results.

There are two important questions for high school teachers. First, how do we know when someone has taken down a mammoth? Second, how do we celebrate, document, and practice this move so everyone begins to take down mammoths? Schools must implement strong metrics for college and workforce readiness, place proven programs in the hands of teachers, provide them training on twenty-first century learning, and organize time for professionals to work in teams with incentives to produce results.

# PART III

*"I think a major act of leadership right now,
call it a radical act, is to create the places and processes
so people can actually learn together, using our experiences."*

MARGARET J. WHEATLEY

When I first started to think about the research high school concept, I thought a great deal about medicine. I went to every research hospital website I could find. I talked to research hospital administrators and tried to reflect on my work through their experiences. I realized that medicine had a mechanism in place (the research hospital) that could be translated to education (specifically high schools). This idea had the potential to develop social capital in a network of schools, and in turn be a strategy for civic and economic development. The research high school like the research hospital is a key regional economic development strategy that begins with the investment of research and development and ends with a stronger economy.

INVEST R&D → NEW PRACTICE RESULTS → STRONGER WORKFORCE → ATTRACT/ BUILD NEW INDUSTRIES → NEW TAX REVENUE TO INVEST

When I went to MD Anderson's website and clicked on "research," I found these words: "MD Anderson's history is filled with stories of physicians, scientists, and others who observed a problem and worked to solve it." The teamwork approach to drive solutions in medicine reflected my aspirations in education. I began to compare medicine and education.

| Medicine (Research Hospital) | Education (Research High School) |
|---|---|
| *People Business* | *People Business* |
| *Wellness Relationships* | *Learning Relationships* |
| *More patient responsibility, better results* | *More student responsibility, better results* |
| *Struggle with data management: need the right real time data at point of decisions* | *Struggle with data management: need the right real time data at point of decisions* |
| *Professional practitioners who are trained with theory and proven programs in residencies* | *Professional practitioners who are trained with theory and thrown to the wolves* |
| *Differentiated patient care with new roles like nurse practitioners* | *Just starting to more effectively use different roles like instructional interventionists* |
| *Huge R&D money* | *No R&D Money* |
| *Research Hospitals Drive New Practice* | *No Research High Schools Driving Practice* |
| *Innovation spreads like wildfire* | *Innovation is a series of isolated campfires* |

I didn't come to my position as a high school principal thinking, "I am going to build the research high school." So how did I arrive at this place to write about this concept? I do know the following things about myself that seemed to lead me to create some definition around this work: I know that I can't sleep at night because I am always thinking I need to find more solutions to serve more kids better. I know I run hard, I am never satisfied, and I ask questions that need to be addressed through data, not emotions. I know I love people; I like to stand outside and talk to parents picking up their kids and wave to folks as they come and go. I know I like to talk to kids at lunch and use the time between classes to test ideas out on faculty. I know, unfortunately, when I come near teachers they often cringe and think, "Please don't make me think between classes." I know what they think about me, and I'm the first to laugh at my obsessive behavior.

The research high school concept germinated from the leadership team at Crown Point High School. It is a direction. It is an approach. It is a philosophy. It is a way you do business. It also requires like-minded, talented people all down the line who buy into this philosophy. We are going to consistently ask questions, test ideas, and try new things to get better results for more kids.

The link between medicine and education is very clear and transferable in many areas. We took MD Anderson's clear thinking and simple mission—"We Cure Cancer"—into our mission work. Our latest mission statement is modeled after many of the powerful research hospital examples like MD Anderson. Our new mission is: *Creating Possibilities, Ensuring Success, and Inspiring Character: A promise to help all students achieve beyond their potential!* By the way, it was a student leader who came up with the word "beyond," which I love.

My hope in the last section of this book is to provide the reader with a way of thinking about regional economic development through the work of the research high school. There are three essential components that are defined in the final chapters.

First, the research high school is modeled after the research hospital. This work is defined through a new set of frameworks, roles, and practices.

Secondly, the research high school is not a stand-alone institution. It has to be part of a larger regional network of high schools that are committed to powerful new outcomes. This network has to be built on a solid infrastructure in order to quickly share practices that produce better results for kids and communities.

Thirdly, public education will not reinvent itself from within. A regional economic development structure that works outside of the system is essential to place the right pressure and influence on the system to produce the results we need as regions, states, and a country to be competitive in a new global economy.

These three big ideas are visually represented below. The research high school is the focal point of regional economic development to drive a stronger workforce. This big industry influence on the work of schools creates the right pressure and relationships to build a system of continuous improvement. The graphic also represents a new type of structure. New structures like the relationship presented below are critical to produce new results.

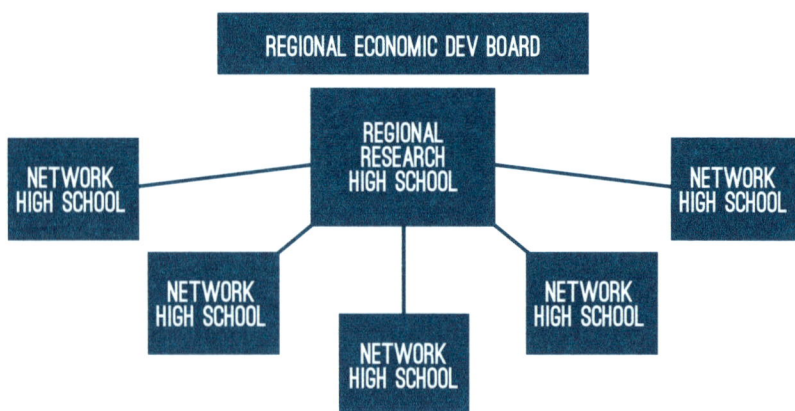

Billions of dollars have been spent on high school reform with very little systemic fundamental changes and new sustainable results. The last section of this book maps a new way to drive sustainable improvement that will produce better results for the population of fourteen to eighteen-year-old students in this country. A regional investment in the best high schools, as research sites, is the only hope to drive innovation through a system that functions as if we are still in the Industrial Revolution. Let's move the American public high school away from the assembly line and into the new competitive global economy.

# CHAPTER SEVEN

*"In the long history of humankind, those who learned
to collaborate and improvise most effectively have prevailed."*

CHARLES DARWIN

How do you hire people? How do you help folks identify problems? How do you know which problems to work on and how to apply your resources? I asked so many questions when I spoke with the research hospital administrators. I came to realize that my work developing a research high school was not much different. We have a ton of similarities on personnel, budgeting, and how to get our arms around all the data we collect. The talented research hospital administrators helped me to understand that we are working in a new type of leadership space. My dad used to say that if you are not consistently changing and improving, people are passing you by. Leading in a culture of continuous improvement is actually what my best teachers do with their kids. They inspire, invent, and produce better results every year.

It was helpful to review documents, frameworks, and processes that take place in the research hospital. This made me walk back through our planning and developmental processes at Crown Point to recreate the breakthrough concept Systems of Innovation. All of the pieces seemed to emerge together through the course of three years of work until I meticulously walked back through each step. There is a distinct flow to the *Systems of Innovation*. I will briefly share how each piece developed and provide examples to help construct a complete picture of how the system flows. Then I will provide a few examples of innovation.

***Systems of Innovation Flow:***

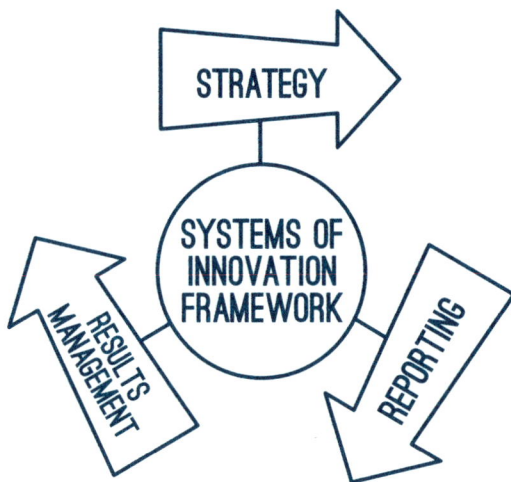

***Framework: Defining the Sandbox***

At the center of this concept is the framework. The current systems of innovation framework includes the elements of our approach to school transformation: freshman transitions, twenty-first century learning, and college and career programming. It seems simple and relevant. It was not so clear in the beginning.

This is the very brief story of how we arrived at this framework. Everyone always wants to know from the new principal "Where are we going?" How could I be a good role model to teachers if I answered all their questions directly? I wanted my staff to be critical professional thinkers that worked together to solve problems and define our direction. Ignore the urge to give your faculty answers to questions if you want them to engage and collaboratively own the direction of the school. Okay, I didn't completely ignore the question. I just came up with a simple visual and a challenge in the fall of my first year as principal. The faculty wanted and needed some direction, and I thought that was fair. I was insistent that the direction of the school was to be developed as a whole organization. I was just the editor of this faculty-driven work.

At one faculty meeting at the end of the first semester in fall, 2008, I shared a new visual. This visual contained some of the best high school re-design topics, Richard Elmore's foundation for school reform (research, best practice, community voice) and Barbara McCombs' student-centered focus, our school improvement agenda, and our newly created values that we called the "portrait of a Crown Point graduate." I asked the faculty to identify areas of interest, and when opportunities emerged, I invited folks to work in those areas. The first systems of innovation visual looked like this:

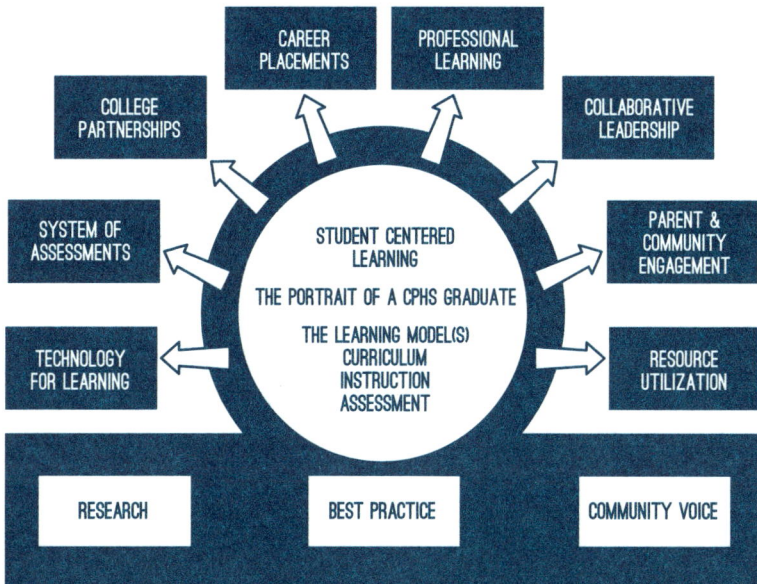

For example, I had been courting our local university leaders (I had the right fishing line in the water). Once they had clearly demonstrated an interest (I had a bite!), and they decided to come to the high school (hooked the fish), I personally invited the faculty who said they were interested in teaching college classes to help prepare for the meeting with our university partners. No extra pay, no issues with meeting outside of the contract. These were people driven by clear interests and passions. We had enough volunteers for anything we wanted to do. We just opened up the concept area, invited people to join in, and bam, it started working.

One big key to this concept is a strong administrative team. When your faculty admires and trusts your assistant principals—wow, what a force multiplier in a school. This is also assuming you have the sense enough to place them in real leadership roles to run with these concepts. I am a big believer in unleashing talent. The initial systems of innovation idea (the visual) really helped to organize and channel the work for my administrative leadership team.

Using the framework that emerged (the initial systems of innovation visual), we began an exciting journey, and I began to track everything into a project plan. Everything we did at the school was categorized under this framework. New student leadership, student mentoring groups, parent leadership groups, a new director of learning technology, ACT

## REFLECTION

The administrative team at the high school was exceptional. They had all the attributes you look for in a highly performing team. They intensely cared about kids and families, they worked hard, they developed trust, and followed through to serve teachers. They were visible and lived in the community.

We all would run into each other on Sundays and at all hours of the day and night. Our kids had practices at the high school, and what else is there to do when waiting for your kids to finish practice than go into your office and work?

assessment system, teacher leadership academy, and the list goes on and on. Dream it up, place it in the right project area, and drive it. Without the framework, we were in chaos mode. With the framework, the world made sense to most people. In year one, with a new principal, this framework made sense to the key people who needed some clarity and focus, including many of my closest administrative team leaders.

I am a maniac at matrices and alignment. Here is one small glimpse from the project plan that emerged from the systems of innovation visual. This document went on for pages with status and alignment to goals. I met with each owner to determine if and how we should move forward.

| Breakthrough School Category *Programs* | *Conversations* | *Planning* | *Planning /Pilot* | *Implementing* | *Evaluating* | *F.I.R.E.* | *CPHS Goal 1* | *CPHS Goal 2* | *CPHS Goal 3* | *CPHS Goal 4* | *CPHS Goal 5* | *District Goal 1* | *District Goal 2* | *District Goal 3* | *Owner* |
|---|---|---|---|---|---|---|---|---|---|---|---|---|---|---|---|
| **System of Assessments** | | | | | | | | | | | | | | | |
| *ACT EPAS System (8th and 9th grade)* | | | ● | | | F/I | | | ● | | ● | ● | | | *Mark G.* |
| *ACT EPAS System 8th – 11th grade* | | ● | | | | I | | | ● | | ● | | | ● | *Deb C.* |
| *ACT End of Course Assessments* | ● | | | | | I | | | ● | | ● | ● | | | *Deb C.* |
| *Six Weeks Assessments* | | | | ● | | I | | | ● | | | | | | *Deb C.* |
| *8th Grade RTI Student Risk Factor Screener* | | ● | | | | F | | | | | | | | ● | *Mark G.* |
| **College Partnerships** | | | | | | | | | | | | | | | |
| *PUC – Core Courses / Engineering / Business* | | ● | | | | I | | | | | ● | | | ● | *Chip P.* |
| *IUN – Medicine / Teacher Ed / Human Services* | | ● | | | | I | | | | | ● | | | ● | *Deb Cioc* |
| *Ivy Tech Partnership CTE* | | ● | | | | I | | | | | ● | | | ● | *Scott R.* |
| *Parent / Student College Planning Services* | | | | ● | | R | ● | | | | | | | | *Guidance* |
| **Career Placements** | | | | | | | | | | | | | | | |
| *ICE Program (Transition of Hero to Business)* | | ● | | | | I | | | | | ● | | ● | | *Mary B.* |

**ЯR** REFLECTION

We did so much surveying early on. We continue to do systematic surveying, and we always provide the information back to the groups we survey.

The development of our direction was truly a community endeavor. I am sure that many people just looked at all the activity as busy work. I really looked at the effort to engage the entire community as vital to our growth and development.

I believe that the majority of people respect the effort involved in listening.

My purpose for displaying some of the early detailed work is to show that the eventual high school framework emerged from intense and detailed work that aligned with every element from our strategic plan called FIRE (Freshman, Instruction, Relationships, Environment) to every school and district goal. We meticulously surveyed everyone during this process. The student voice was extremely important. As you can see from this artifact, students were asked to rate the impact of the proposed activity—the activity here was developing college and career partnerships for the school—the kids clearly voted that college and career programs were our number one priority. Richard Elmore's part of the systems of innovation visual is extremely important (community voice). The kids spoke clearly.

College & Career Partnerships

A    4% lowest impact

B    0% low impact

C    4% moderate impact

D    44% high impact

E    48% highest impact

In strategic planning sessions with the administrative team, it was obvious that our systems of innovation visual needed further simplification. We needed a stronger and more laser-like focus on the new work of high schools. For an entire school year we tried to simplify and summarize this work. The breakthrough came to an assistant principal after a year of intense dialog and debate. We finally repositioned everything under three simple ideas: freshman transitions, twenty-first century learning, and college and career programming. We had our framework. This framework defined the pipeline that served our fourteen to eighteen-year-olds. This framework is now the simple framework for our *Systems of Innovation* work. And it has been adopted by forty other schools.

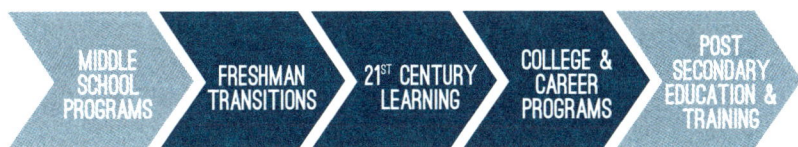

MIDDLE SCHOOL PROGRAMS → FRESHMAN TRANSITIONS → 21ˢᵀ CENTURY LEARNING → COLLEGE & CAREER PROGRAMS → POST SECONDARY EDUCATION & TRAINING

Having frameworks is helpful, but the faculty needed to be introduced to the new framework through storytelling, or as we called it, a "destination post card." So we built a brochure. For three years we have been telling the same story about where we are going, and it has helped drive a stronger focus to the work while allowing for more creative strategies to surface inside this simple framework. Innovative organizations have structure and frameworks. Here, I have provided our framework and the unique school narrative that is the foundation for our Systems of Innovation.

*Crown Point brochure, used by 40+ schools*

### Engage: Freshman Transitions

Incoming students engage in a whole school culture that supports their social, personal, and academic growth.

A baseline of college readiness is established for every eighth-grade student through the ACT Explore assessment. ACT Explore reports are presented to students and parents to help guide freshman programming. Parents, students, and faculty teams meet over the school year to determine individualized learning plans and technology-based interventions and acceleration pathways.

Freshmen are assigned senior student mentors to engage them in extra and co-curricular programs. Students work on core skill development and cross-curricular projects in team settings. Additionally, students develop power skills like time management and information literacy while they explore careers and plan for post-secondary programming. All freshmen conclude the year with the ACT Plan assessment and ACT Work Keys to measure individual growth and to determine placement into college and career programs based on college and career readiness.

Every student concludes the freshman year with a plan and pathway that includes rigorous high school programs and post-secondary education and training. Pathways lead students to the best emerging careers.

Freshman Transition Strategies

+ Parent orientation
+ Student orientation
+ ACT Formative and Summative Assessments and Reports
+ Faculty teams
+ Core academic skill development
+ Individualized math and reading acceleration
+ Cross-curricular project-based learning
+ Senior student mentor program
+ Extra- and co-curricular recruitment and rush activities
+ Power skill development
+ College planning and admissions
+ Career exploration

### *Experience: Twenty-first Century Learning*

Students experience rigorous and relevant programs that use emerging technologies to develop critical thinking for a competitive global world.

Academic programming is articulated to certification and degree programs with participating university partners. Complementing this programming is a strong comprehensive set of elective programs in language, culture, communications, and arts to allow students to explore and pursue interests.

Differentiated learning models and the use of digital content meet the unique needs of each student. Online, blended, credit recovery, and skill development courses and experiences are Web-based and available for students twenty-four hours a day, seven days a week. Communication tools allow real time progress monitoring for students, parents, and faculty.

Students experience high impact teaching strategies (HITS) to increase retention of critical knowledge and skills. Students are also assigned an advisor in their career field to help with college and career planning. CPHS commits professional time and resources for faculty training and collaboration on research-based instructional strategies, emerging learning technologies, and advisory.

Students are assessed on college and workforce readiness with the ACT Plan, the ACT, and ACT Work Keys. The longitudinal data is used to measure student growth on college and career readiness. Teacher teams (PLCs, or professional learning communities) use the data to improve instruction.

Twenty-First Century Learning Programs and Strategies

- ⇥ ACT College and workforce readiness standards
- ⇥ ACT Formative and Summative Assessments and Reports
- ⇥ One laptop, one student plan
- ⇥ Technology infrastructure plan

- Learning management solution
- Blended and fully online instructional models
- Digital skill development programs
- Reading interventions
- Digital credit recovery labs
- Curriculum-based scheduling
- College and career advisors
- Faculty training (assessment, technology integration, PLC, PBL, HITS)
- Instructional coaching
- PLC (professional learning communities)
- PBL (project-based learning)
- HITS (high impact teaching strategies)

### *Excel: College and Career Partnerships*

Students excel in college and career programs by successfully attaining job training, certifications, and college credits.

Based on a powerful new model of college and career programming, students have unprecedented access to Advanced Placement courses, state university programs, and community college career and technical programs. All college-equivalent course experiences are measured for validity and reliability. Advanced Placement exams, common university midterms and final exams, and industry certifications are validated. University faculty oversees program quality through a next-generation learning system and inter-rater scoring protocols. Inter-rater scoring for the university programs generates student outcome data to drive faculty and teacher professional dialogue to improve instruction.

What is learned is applied at CPHS. Students excel through internships and capstone experiences in their fields of study. Additional partners include community agencies and businesses to challenge students to contribute to the economic and social growth of the community. Students complete their high school careers by documenting their social impact on the local community through a required forty hours of community service.

College and Career Programs and Strategies

- ✦ Advanced Placement courses
- ✦ Dual credit courses
- ✦ Industry certifications
- ✦ Internships and job placement services
- ✦ Internship and capstone placement model
- ✦ Community service projects

*© 2011 Crown Point H.S.*

## *Reporting—The Scoreboard*

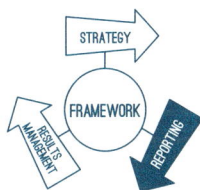

After the middle section of the Systems of Innovation flow was defined the first way to move the organization forward we had to define a clear way of reporting results. As I talked with my hospital administrator colleagues, there was a pronounced gap between the work and how we reported the work at the high school. We had no scoreboard that energized people and tracked the right data. Sure we had state test scores, but no one cares about state standards and school accountability besides the principals and maybe the math and

### ℝ REFLECTION

We have a great story to tell. Many schools have taken notice of our simple framework and story. As we begin to use common metrics for college and workplace readiness and common learning systems to manage our data, our research high school can help to identify the strategies in a network of schools that are producing the best results, and spread those innovations like wildfire across the network.

This framework and story are key strategies for sharing innovative practice. The schools that are using the framework find it very simple and focused.

English teachers. During the first two years, we had monthly faculty meetings where we presented every relevant data piece we could collect. The teachers began to see that we measured everything and presented it back to them. Here is a simple piece of data from our Freshman Transitions goal in year two.

*Goal 3: Freshman Transitions*

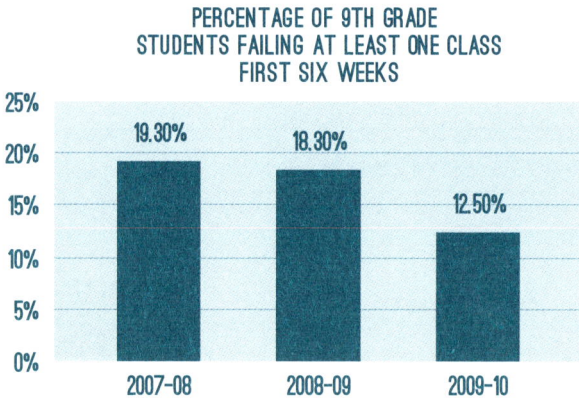

**PERCENTAGE OF 9TH GRADE STUDENTS FAILING AT LEAST ONE CLASS FIRST SIX WEEKS**

| Year | Percentage |
|------|-----------|
| 2007-08 | 19.30% |
| 2008-09 | 18.30% |
| 2009-10 | 12.50% |

After three years of maintaining the same five organizational goals, we began to track the right metrics and indicators to see our trends. The faculty began to see what we were going to track and report as a school. We began to set goals at every level and measure those goals. The administrative team took the lead to set the example of accountability. For example, each assistant principal began to own a section of the systems of innovation framework—freshman transitions, twenty-first century learning, college and career programming. We then developed specific goals to measure the success of our strategies. Everything was measured and our goals were in the hands of the faculty. We were all accountable and we would begin to report our data in a more systematic and routine way. The following outlines how we set goals to generate the data.

## *2010 / 2011 School Goals*

- → Attendance: Increase attendance rate
- → Environment: Increase C-Notes and decrease discipline referrals
- → Freshman Transitions: Increase freshman college readiness rates and decrease course failures
- → Twenty-first century learning: Increase college and career readiness in all ACT categories
- → College and career programming: Increase the number of college level courses completed

## *2010 / 2011 Administrative Leadership Team Goals*

Assistant Principal—Freshman Principal

- → Increase positive student behaviors to 15,000 C-Notes and decrease discipline referrals
- → Increase freshman college and career readiness
- → Reduce freshmen failures
- → Guidance Team: ninety-eight percent attendance rate, 5,000 C-Notes, fifty percent academic honors, and thirty percent technical honors

Assistant Principal—Academic programming and twenty-first century learning

- → Increase college readiness in tenth and eleventh grade plan and ACT
- → Increase AP test taking and passing rates to twenty percent of graduating seniors earning a three or better on an AP test
- → Reduce tenth to twelfth grade course failures through response to intervention
- → Guidance Team: ninety-seven percent attendance rate, ninety-four percent graduation rate, 4,000 C-Notes, thirty-five percent academic honors, twenty percent technical honors, and seventy percent college attainment

Assistant Principal—Strategy and College and Career Partnerships

→ 5.000 college credits earned, seventy-five percent of senior class graduate with college credit

→ Guidance Team: ninety-seven percent attendance rate, ninety-four percent graduation rate, 4,000 C-Notes, thirty-five percent academic honors, twenty percent technical honors, and seventy percent college attainment

As we became clear about our goals and metrics around our framework, we were able to move into reporting our trends routinely to our entire community. The community loved the quarterly report we developed in year three as part of our commitment to improving our communication strategies. Here is a section from Goal Five—College and Career Programming.

## GOAL 5: COLLEGE AND CAREER PROGRAMMING

**Increase the number of college level courses completed.**

*Crown Point High School has dramatically increased access to rigorous college courses to meet the needs of all students.*

*Advanced Placement participation and performance continues to accelerate along with state university and community college career and technical courses. The projected advanced placement and dual credit completion rates are helping more students to accelerate their degree completion. In addition, the development of an affordable state university dual credit model has provided families real access to Big Ten University credits at 80% reduction in cost.*

### STUDENTS SERVED BY ADVANCED PLACEMENT PROGRAMMING

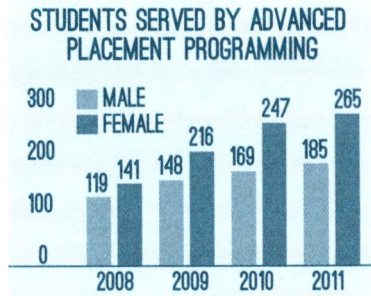

*The graph represents the four year trends in the number of students served by Advanced Placement programming by gender.*

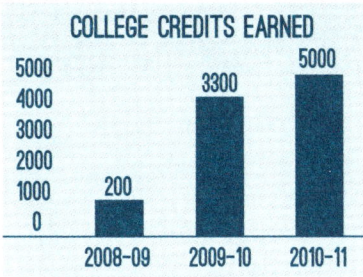

### COLLEGE CREDITS EARNED

*The graph represents the number of college credits earned through Indiana University Northwest, Purdue University Calumet, and Ivy Tech State College.*

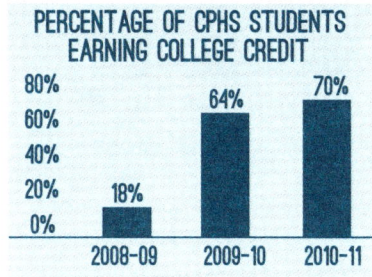

### PERCENTAGE OF CPHS STUDENTS EARNING COLLEGE CREDIT

*The graph represents the 3 year trend in the percentage of students who graduate with a 3 on an AP score and/or at least 3 college credits earned.*

You can see that our framework helped us to focus our data, which told the story about the shift toward serving all kids better over time. The reporting of our data became our first driver in the systems of innovation flow. The wheel started to move. It is important to note that there are many qualitative and cultural (affective) parts to the work of high schools. I am making some assumptions in this book that people know how to improve school culture while the organization is evolving. Thus, my focus here is the data, but the people always come first and we maintained strong relationships through all this work.

### *Results Management—The New Personnel Management*

After we began reporting and providing better data pictures, working with people became focused on the results we were trying to achieve

If you talk with many high school leaders, they will share that they feel like the ringmaster at the big top. At a comprehensive high school it can feel like a circus.

Teachers, like any profession, want a relevant and fair way evaluate their work. I will go back to the infrastructure idea here. We continue to work with

*continued on page 86*

*continued from page 85*

## REFLECTION

some national assessment leaders to construct better real-time data strategies for high school teachers to have results at their fingertips to help them manage learning. We all want clarity in our work. We all want good information. We all will play the right game hard if we are valued in this work.

Managing results is a much more objective way to look at the work "with" a teacher. I can ask what do you think about these results? If I don't have results, then I am working on judgments and emotions. The judgment and emotion game simply perpetuates the circus.

with kids. Thus, I refer to this part of the flow as results management. Managing people without good data is really hard work. Managing results is a much better way to get things done in a complex environment.

The framework was set, the reports began to flow, and the data provided a more clear way of defining roles and goals in the system. How many people in a high school have a clear job description and know the power metrics they need to hit with accuracy? Below is our administrative organization chart so you can see the whole administrative team. The first three roles for the assistant principals are 100 percent aligned to our framework.

### ADMINISTRATIVE LEADERSHIP ORGANIZATIONAL CHART

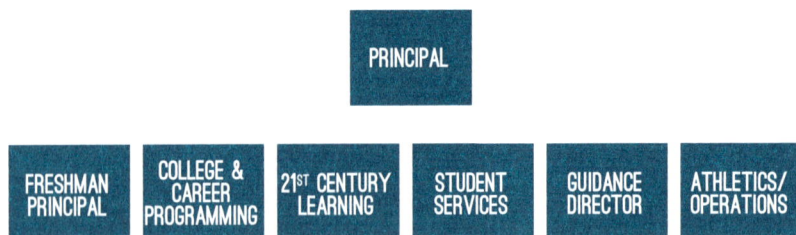

PRINCIPAL

FRESHMAN PRINCIPAL | COLLEGE & CAREER PROGRAMMING | 21ST CENTURY LEARNING | STUDENT SERVICES | GUIDANCE DIRECTOR | ATHLETICS/OPERATIONS

Now, since I used the reporting example from the college and career programming part of the school framework, let me share with you the job description of the assistant principal that owns college and career programming so you can see how I positioned the results management through clarity in job functions.

### *Assistant Principal: College and Career Programming*

Organizational responsibilities

→ Academic partnerships

Manage college partnership project plan

Construct Pathways with College Partners

Develop college partnership "playbook" for state

→ Strategy and Accountability

Establish organizational growth needs and manage teacher leadership work

Develop and deliver routine school data reports for multiple uses

Develop overarching program evaluation plan and timeline for school (including all surveys, focus groups, etc.)

Set and attain yearly school award targets

→ Assessment

Meet with district director of curriculum and assessment to set performance targets

Implement state testing plan

Implement ACT EPAS testing system

Generate reports for instructional interventions

→ Summer School

Develop and run summer school

Functional responsibilities

→ District

- Secondary assessment specialist

→ School

- Academic partnerships
- Teacher leadership
- Assessment
- Summer school
- Attends administrative leadership meetings
- Attends instructional leadership meetings

- Supervises buses, lunch, extra-, co-, and curricular activities
- Attendance and discipline for twenty-five percent of students

Area reporting and evaluation responsibilities

- ↪ Dual credit and assessment secretary
- ↪ Dual credit faculty
- ↪ CTE Faculty
- ↪ Department reports and support evaluations
  1. Industrial Technology department
  2. FACS Department
  3. Business Department
- ↪ Guidance counselor
- ↪ Office of Workforce Development

Individual and administrative power goals and metrics

- ↪ Increase college-level course equivalents successfully completed by fifty percent
- ↪ Establish and attain school award targets (regional, state, national)
- ↪ Effective execution of all testing programs

Administrative and counselor power goals for 2010/2011

- ↪ Ninety-seven percent attendance rate
- ↪ Seventy percent of graduates earn college course equivalency or industry certification
- ↪ Ninety-four percent graduation rate

Yearly work products and tasks

- ↪ Data dashboard (quarterly and end-of-year report)
- ↪ College partnership playbook, project plan, and project management
- ↪ College pathways planning guides
- ↪ Summer school plan and materials
- ↪ College and career programming section of strategic plan
- ↪ Reports on longitudinal assessments and state assessments
- ↪ Develop and maintain Web site for college attainment and

summer school

+ Yearly testing calendar

+ All testing reports and requirements

Professional Responsibilities

+ Set individual learning agenda aligned to organizational areas

+ Attends conferences

+ Presents at conferences

+ Write and publish dual credit work

Results management is a critical concept! This work started with the administrative team and it is starting to work its way down through the system. I work intensely with administrative team on co-constructing their job descriptions each summer. They know what they own. They are the right people in the right seats. I take great care in working with them individually and collectively to identify their passions, interests, and talents. They are now specialists in their field due to their laser-focused results management work. I always come back to the need for infrastructure. The stronger and more comprehensive the assessment picture and learning system, the better we will be at managing our results for kids with everyone from the administrative team, faculty, students, and parents.

### *Strategy—Direction and Focus*

As I continued my conversations with the hospital folks, I realized that school people did not do strategy well. We operate in the same space and traditionally manage what we have. In our defense, there is very little time to do anything else, given the structure of most high schools. But we had to be different.

Many people ask why I talk about strategic planning last. I like to measure first and know what I have before I come up with strategies. For example, the C-Note program identified that we had a disengagement issue. I had a hunch, but I really didn't know until we measured.

Once we knew the data, we began to implement adult mentors, student mentoring, student club rush activities, and other focused strategies that promoted and drove a higher level of engagement in the organization.

There is a flow, and the three pieces of reporting, results management, and strategy all overlap. I just prefer to measure, control, adjust and measure again.

We took time to work through strategic planning. We did our best on convening parents, students, businesses, higher education, faculty, etc. We hosted drum circles for team building and talked. After we talked, we charted, we surveyed, and we planned our future together. Each year we revisit our one-page strategic plan and update it. The plan is built around our framework. Everything is tightly connected through job descriptions and power goals.

The strategic planning completes the Systems of Innovation flow. We have intense ownership in the main areas of the framework. You read in the job description of the assistant principal who owns college and career programming and see that person is responsible for strategic planning in that area, setting goals, and managing results. Each assistant principal comes to me for resources, guidance, and support. The strategic plan is posted in every hallway, every classroom, and in every faculty directory. It is our guiding document, and nothing happens unless it is on the strategic plan. It is dense, but it fits on one page. When I was a teacher, I used to allow my chemistry students to write anything they wanted on a five-by-eight-inch note card and bring it into the test. The process of them constructing that note card was more valuable than testing them. Get your plans down in a simple way so it is accessible to everyone. On the following pages are the elements of our strategy: each part of the framework – freshman transitions, twenty-first century learning, college and career programming, and student support services all tailored and personalized for each family and student.

## DISCOVERY: STRATEGIC PLAN 2011 – 2012

| FRESHMEN: *Transition programming for all freshmen to develop social, personal, and academic skills required to succeed in high school* | 2010–11 | 2011–12 | 2012–13 | 2013–14 |
|---|---|---|---|---|
| **College & Career Exploration & Planning** *(ACT Explore)* | ▪ | ▪ | ▪ | |
| **Power Skills** *(Teamwork, Study Skills, Time Management, Character Education, Financial and Information Literacy)* | ▪ | ▪ | ▪ | ▪ |
| **Academic Houses** *(Integrated Planning, Student Cohort Groups, Professional Learning communities)* | ▪ | ▪ | ▪ | ▪ |
| **Student / Parent Orientation** *(Middle School Visits, Bulldog Rush, Freshman Parent Night, Extended Orientation Activities, Parent Cohort Groups)* | ▪ | ▪ | ▪ | |
| **Learning Interventions** *(Math and Literacy Labs, Response to Intervention, Intensive Algebra Curriculum, Summer School Programming, Biology Transition, Policies to ensure support and success)* | ▪ | ▪ | ▪ | ▪ |
| **6-12 Vertical Articulation** *(6th Grade Graduation Plans, Course Sequencing Models, College Readiness, Middle School-High School Faculty Collaboration)* | ▪ | ▪ | ▪ | ▪ |
| **TOP DOG Mentoring** *(Senior Mentors and Teaching Assistants)* | ▪ | ▪ | ▪ | |

COLOR BAR CODE: Research ▪ Plan ▪ Pilot ▪
Implement ▪ Evaluate ▪ Abandon

| TWENTY-FIRST CENTURY LEARNING: *Rigorous and relevant programming for all students to become critical thinkers succeeding in a competitive global world* | 2010-11 | 2011-12 | 2012-13 | 2013-14 |
|---|---|---|---|---|
| **Academic Relevance** *(ACT College Standards, AP College Board Standards, Workplace Readiness Standards, Common Core Standards, Quality Core Standards)* | Research | Pilot | Implement | Evaluate |
| **Learning Relationships** *(Teaching Teamwork, Student Communication, Parent Communication, Office Hours like Zero Period to build faculty/student relationships)* | Research | Pilot | Pilot | Evaluate |
| **Comprehensive Assessments** *(Formative, Nine Weeks, End of Course, ACT EPAS, PSAT, SAT, Quality Core, and Authentic Assessments)* | Research | Pilot | Implement | Evaluate |
| **High Impact Instructional Strategies** *(Inquiry, Research, Cooperative Learning, Practice, Non-Linguistic Representations, Reinforcement, Similarities and Differences, Content Literacy, Project-Based Learning)* | Plan | Implement | Evaluate | Evaluate |
| **Individual Learning Plans** *(Technology-Based tools to organize learning data for students, parents, faculty, and staff that drive individual student learning plans including literacy labs, math labs, learning center support, academic advising)* | Research | Pilot | Evaluate | Evaluate |
| **Digital Learning Opportunities** *(Web-Based Digital Curriculum, Credit Recovery, Technology-Enhanced Instruction, On-Line Classes, Blended Learning)* | Pilot | Implement | Evaluate | |
| **Technology Access** *(Computer Labs, Computer Carts, One-to-One Technology Plan)* | Research | Plan | Pilot | Implement |
| **Learning Structure** *(Modified Schedule, Standards-Based Grading & Reporting, Digital Courseware, Teaming for students in need)* | Research | Pilot | Implement | Evaluate |
| **Professional Development** *(BrainHoney, Project-Based Learning, Instructional Coaching, Relationship Training, Diversity Training, New Teacher Induction, Content Literacy, Data-Driven Instruction, Formative Assessments)* | Pilot | Implement | Evaluate | |
| **Professional Learning Communities PLC** *Common Projects, Formative & Summative Assessments, Curriculum Maps, Routinely Used Formative Data to Change Instruction to meet the Learning Needs of every student* | Pilot | Implement | Evaluate | |

**COLOR BAR CODE:** Research ▮ Plan ▮ Pilot ▮ Implement ▮ Evaluate ▮ Abandon

| COLLEGE AND CAREER PROGRAMMING: *Aligned and effective college and career programs* | 2010-11 | 2011-12 | 2012-13 | 2013-14 |
|---|---|---|---|---|
| **College and Career Partnerships** *(Dual Credit - Purdue University Calumet, Indiana University Northwest, Ivy Tech)* | Pilot | Implement | Evaluate | |
| **Assessment** *(ACT EPAS & Quality Core, PSAT & SAT, AP, ASVAB, Work Keys/COMPASS, Dept. of Ed. End-of-Course Assessments, Certification Exams, College Placement Exams)* | Pilot | Implement | | |
| **Career Pathways** *(Individual Road Maps for all students aligned with AP, Dual Credit, and Core Transfer Library, Cohorts of students in Common Pathways with faculty advisor)* | Plan | Pilot | Implement | Evaluate |
| **Career Placements** *(Workforce Development Internships and Capstone Projects)* | Research | Plan | Pilot | Implement |

| LEADERSHIP BY RELATIONSHIPS: *A system and plan to ensure that all students, parents, faculty, and staff are connected through healthy and productive relationships* | 2010-11 | 2011-12 | 2012-13 | 2013-14 |
|---|---|---|---|---|
| **Faculty Advisory** *(Advise, Counsel, and Mentor Students in life, academic, career, and post-secondary planning)* | Research | Plan | Pilot | Implement |
| **Student Mentoring** *(Top Dogs, Peer Tutors, CASS Cadets, Student Crisis Team, Comprehensive New Student Support)* | Pilot | Plan | Implement | Evaluate |
| **Positive Learning Environment** *(Positive Behavior Incentives, Students of the Week, C-Note, Drug and Alcohol Programming, Crisis Training, Security Plan, Handbook Policies, Respect Initiative)* | Evaluate | Implement | Evaluate | Evaluate |
| **Faculty & Staff Leadership** *(Faculty Leadership Incentives, New Teacher Induction, Professional Learning Communities, Social Events, Faculty Celebrations)* | Research | Pilot | Implement | Evaluate |
| **Student Leadership** *(LEAD Council, Student Council, Athletic Council, ROTC, Principal's Advisory Group)* | Evaluate | Evaluate | Implement | Evaluate |
| **Parent Leadership** *(Parent Ambassadors, Parent Leadership Team, Parent Surveys, Parent Education)* | Evaluate | Evaluate | Implement | Evaluate |
| **CPHS School-Wide Leadership Council** *(Students, Faculty, Parents, Administration, Community Planning for a One-to-One Environment)* | Research | Plan | Pilot | Implement |
| **Effective Communication Strategies** *(Website, Phone, Emails, Videos, Mailings)* | Implement | Implement | Implement | |

COLOR BAR CODE: Research | Plan | Pilot
Implement | Evaluate | Abandon

| STUDENT SERVICES: *Individual plans for each student and family* | 2010–11 | 2011–12 | 2012–13 | 2013–14 |
|---|---|---|---|---|
| **Learning Policies** *(Academic Policies that support academic achievement goals, student post-secondary goals, and Distinguished Graduate designation)* | | | | |
| **Comprehensive Counseling Services** *(College & Career Planning, Social Work, Student EAP, Divorce, Bullying, Death/Loss, Diversity, Depression, Substance Abuse)* | | | | |
| **Individualized Success Plan** *(College Planning, Academic Advising, Parent Communication, Technology Tools)* | | | | |
| **Community Outreach** *(Community Agency support, Community Foundation planning)* | | | | |
| **Alumni Association** *(History, Networks, Support, Mentoring, Retiree Events)* | | | | |

COLOR BAR CODE: Research    Plan    Pilot
Implement    Evaluate    Abandon

### Research and Development in Action

Defining the framework for the Systems of Innovation and then developing the flow around that framework are the two key concepts for creating new practice and producing new results. This understanding is the foundation for the research high school. You might be reflecting at this moment and thinking, "Eric, this all sounds like good strong management stuff, but where are your examples of innovation? How does the R& D actually work?" I love good questions, so let me share a couple stories.

*Innovation Example 1:* A new model of dual credit that changed state policy and received national recognition.

In our relationship with our college partners, we developed a set of assumptions and requirements for a new model of dual credit. We were going to move from a retail to a wholesale approach to college programming. The high school had the facility and faculty. The colleges had the programming. We just had to figure out how to scale this work and create a distribution model that increased quality, increased access, and decreased cost. We knew that we had to beat the competition on quality if we were going to dramatically change the paradigm. In the game of higher education, where reputation and credentials rule, we were going to produce something that very few had—measurable results.

We worked closely with Agilix Labs developing a powerful new learning system called BrainHoney. We had intense debates on how to scale quality. We came up with the idea that we would deliver common assessments and build an inter-rater scoring technology in partnership with our regional universities.. Every physics midterm and final would be the same on campus and in our classrooms. These exams would be delivered through the learning system, and there would be constructed response items that would need to be graded by our teachers. The learning system would randomly select a percentage of the assessments, and the college faculty would grade

## REFLECTION

I share stories of innovation with the qualifying statement that sometimes, when innovating, you are flying by the seat of your pants. These are new things, and new things take a risk tolerance. My administrative team is awesome. We take great care in reducing the risk for our kids and families while we step out to figure out how to serve them better.

For example, when working with the universities to provide lower cost college programming, we were in the eleventh hour in many situations where we had to tell parents a price that we did not even have yet. The innovation work is tough stuff, but it is fun for hunters.

When developing a relationship with one of our local university partners, I was working with our English department chair, who was doing her leadership internship with me. I had her prepare some things for the meeting and before the meeting she was confident. I had to lean over and tell her, "Don't assume that I actually have a plan." A look of shock came over her face, and then a smile. At that moment she understood that innovation is exploration.

Letter from 2011 Crown Point Graduate Lauren Cain:

*Upon entering high school, students' biggest worries include what colleges they will get into, what college they will end up going to, what they will study, if they will be prepared enough for their area of study. By most students' senior year at Crown Point High School, these worries fall away, as it is evident that they have been prepared as one could possibly be. At least, that's how I know it was for me.*

*During my years at Crown Point High School, I was challenged to such an extent that I no longer have to worry about whether or not college will be too hard for me. My teachers had expectations of me that I never thought I could reach—yet, they knew I could, and with their help, I did.*

*Dual Credit classes are also a huge thing to take advantage of at Crown Point High School. With some college tuitions reaching $30,000 annually, being able to get some credits out of the way early is a huge benefit.*

*Though CPHS offers Dual Credit courses through Purdue Calumet, Indiana University Northwest, and Ivy Tech, those are not the only colleges that will accept these credits. Most colleges will still accept them, even if they accept them as an elective credit.*

*continued on page 97*

those exams. The learning system would use a formula to compare the grading of the exams. For those math and science nerds like myself I share the formula:

One interpretation of Krippendorff's *alpha* is:

$$\alpha = 1 - \frac{D_{within\ units\ =\ in\ error}}{D_{within\ and\ between\ units\ =\ in\ in\ total}}$$

$\alpha = 1$ indicates perfect reliability

$\alpha = 0$ indicates the absence of reliability. Units and the values assigned to them are statistically unrelated.

$\alpha < 0$ when disagreements are systematic and exceed what can be expected by chance.

College and high school faculty meet to discuss reliability and accuracy in grading. I actually get chills writing this, because when you innovate and drive a new set of results for kids, it is like "the rush" thrill-seekers get when they climb Mount Everest. Not only were our students taking the same assessments as the on-campus students, the assessments were being graded with accuracy and reliability. We knew without a doubt that our students were measurably performing at the college level. People began to take notice and came from all over to learn about this work, which we presented with our university partners at national and international conferences to share. It sounds so simple to business folks—measure stuff consistently—but it sounds like a foreign language to many higher education folks who have never measured any-thing consistently. The Systems of Innovation had to be in place for me, as the research high school administrator, to have the space to work with assistant principals in identifying resources, writing grants, and building part-nerships to spur this new practice.

*Innovation 2:* The First ACT College Readiness Research High School in the Country!

One of the most important things I did was to bring ACT tools into the high school immediately. Measuring college and workforce skills is essential, and without going into a long explanation, basically, ACT has the best measurement tools for our work.

ACT employs some of the most mission-driven, talented people with whom I have ever worked. They are a research company that has kept an arm's length away from in-terpreting their data too much, given their role as the "testing company." We began to load all their data into guerilla spreadsheets that linked every metric to every piece of data we had. We began to paint pictures and see trends in our programming. Why did the kids in summer school actually demon-strate a decrease in their college readiness scores? Why did our honors kids grow so much faster than our general education kids? Why did our sophomore class demonstrate a decrease in college reading levels?

## PERSPECTIVE

*continued from page 96*

*I can sit here all day and talk about all the wonderful things Crown Point High School has to offer when it comes to college preparation but nothing quite proves it like the facts. As for anyone, paying for college is a huge concern. I will be enter-ing University of Indianapolis this fall as a freshman with 28 credits already under my belt from AP tests and Dual Credit Courses. That's more than a semester's worth of credits and an over $28,000 value! Because of my grades at Crown Point, I received an $11,000 merit schol-arship and with the help of the guidance office, I earned over $3,000 in outside scholarships.*

*No student has an excuse to not succeed at CPHS. They provide the best education, a wonderfully supportive faculty, and the tools to succeed at anything one could try. As is evident from my expe-rience, it definitely pays off to be a student at one of the best high schools in the state.*

We then began to rally our faculty around the metrics to code each test question. We linked questions to standards and skills. We identified skill gaps and used those gaps to plan professional development. The skill gaps were presented to every department and course-based team. The teams set goals around improving college and workforce readiness skills. They developed common formative assessments and began to track the skills.

The assistant principal who owned the twenty-first century learning part of our framework drove this work with incredible focus and passion. The school improvement team embraced the challenge to help all students demonstrate stronger college and workforce readiness skills and everyone was pushing in the same direction—to help all kids demonstrate stronger college and workforce readiness.

We sent our new understandings to ACT, and they sent a senior leadership team to Crown Point. After the visit, we developed a new relationship with ACT. We became their first college and workforce readiness research high school in the country. We have a relationship where our kids, parents, and faculty receive big benefits on free product and services while we create new understandings and implementation ideas to benefit the country. Our district leadership has embraced this work, and now this ACT laboratory school concept advanced to the district level to serve students in grades six through twelve. Every month, our secondary schools meet with ACT to plan, discuss implementation ideas, and share new practice and results.

### Think Possible for Innovation

Think Possible: In the mailroom at the high school there are two signs. First, since we are only an hour from South Bend, Indiana, the home of the

University of Notre Dame, we have a sign above the door that every teacher walks through each morning on his or her way to class that says "Teach Like a Champion Today!" The other sign is the Cadet Maxim from West Point. To think that our military leaders live by this code inspires me to always support sending some of our brightest kids to West Point. I often take this sign off the wall and carry it with me into faculty meetings. It truly embodies the environment we have embraced to lead through a culture of innovation.

*Risk more than others think is safe.*

*Care more than others think is wise.*

*Dream more than others think is practical.*

*Expect more than others think is possible.*

# CHAPTER EIGHT

> *"[The Interstate Highway System] was heralded as the greatest*
> *public works project ever. That it was. And it did, as promised,*
> *lead to an America that is more mobile, less plagued by*
> *regional differences, and vastly wealthier than before."*

JUSTIN FOX, FORTUNE, JANUARY 26, 2004

As research hospitals develop new practices for a larger purpose, the research high school has little value if it works in isolation. Chapter Seven told the story of the emerging work of the research high school. Now consider a few key questions: What is the relationship between the research high school and other schools across a region or state? How do high schools work together across districts? What are the policies and other factors that would help to support the stronger collaborative environment for high schools?

There are currently networks of schools that are functioning well. These networks are most often built around a specific model like New Tech High. The implementation of the model is very specific, and the network helps to ensure fidelity. This is a very strong approach to producing results. I think about these networks like a restaurant franchise. New Tech is like Applebee's. For many communities, this is a great restaurant option, but there are many restaurant concepts for many communities. Is there a way to cut across all models and provide the connectivity and support that is needed to drive a new set of college and career readiness results for America? The answer is yes. The breakthrough idea of infrastructure has been routinely presented and discussed throughout this book. This chapter will focus intensely on the infrastructure needs of the new emerging college acceleration network to serve the needs of all restaurant franchises.

The United States has been a leader on rail, roads, shipping, air, space, and energy infrastructure. Commerce travels fast, and distribution and logistics are powerful concepts in our country. It is time to take this concept into high schools. We need to construct the same connectivity and flow of information and data so we can quickly identify practices that produce results and spread that innovation. Many will challenge that high schools are too complex to run on common infrastructure. In the development of our College Acceleration Network we already have New Tech High Schools, Career Academies, Smaller Learning Communities, schools of over 3,000 students and under 400 students, and a host of others. The development of a network with so many diverse schools demonstrates the need and openness to a set of metrics and learning systems that can help accelerate our competitive edge in the world marketplace.

I have organized the infrastructure picture into the following visual. Every network must have a clear purpose, which is positioned in the middle of the visual. Around that purpose is the same framework that was presented in Chapter Seven. This framework is a way to help organize the work of high schools that provides structure, yet respects the rich and complex nature of high schools. Around the outside of the visual you will notice three key concepts: metrics, systems, and management. These will create the infrastructure for educational commerce and innovation to flow and serve our regions, states, and country.

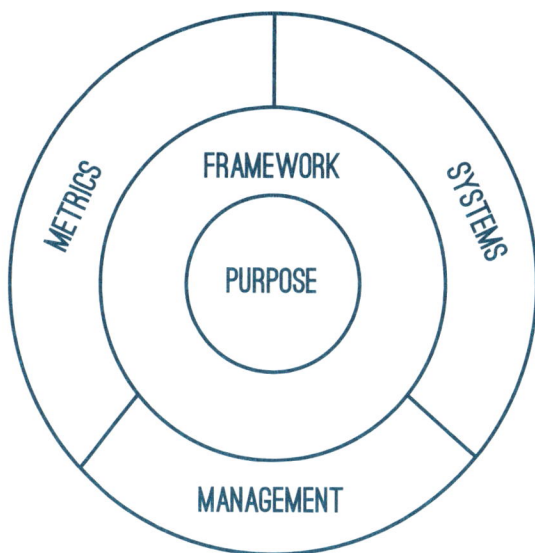

## Purpose and Framework

*The purpose of the College Acceleration Network is to build the infrastructure to accelerate college and career readiness that initiates, rewards, and disseminates innovative practices that produce results.*

This is the new expectation of institutions that serve fourteen to eighteen-year-old students in this country. Yes, I must place a qualifying statement here to recognize that there is a larger context of public schooling. The educational purpose to build caring communities through democratic values and principles is always at the heart of our work. I have provided values-based examples throughout the book. Schools, students, parents, and school boards have run schools for years that promote the values we seek in our students. What these groups have not done is effectively accelerated college and career readiness aligned to regional economic development. Thus, the focus of this chapter is to help provide the support for this work in a more systematic and effective way.

*The framework for the college acceleration network (which also is the framework for our concept of Systems of Innovations for high schools)*

→ *Freshman transitions*

→ *Twenty-first century learning*

→ *College and career programming*

Every high school that joins the network is accepting the framework and applying the principles to the work. This framework is the cornerstone of Systems of Innovation that is now taking place in our network. Schools are telling their stories through this framework. The stories provide a context and promote effective strategies that are being used in the network.

One example is on the freshman transitions work. Many schools have a dedicated freshman principal who is driving stronger programming to help more students better transition into high school. When these principals share their work in the network, they begin to see the key strategies that are producing results. They begin to more easily share with one another the practices that produce results. The practices that produce results then become more common, more quickly in the network.

The framework has empowered our network schools to share their own unique stories. When you are forced to tell your story in a simple and clear way, you quickly focus on the practices that produce results. Through this simple storytelling process, network schools have already shared strategies that have been rapidly implemented across multiple sites to produce better results for kids. The complexities of high schools have to be respected and embraced; this framework is helping to do just that. The purpose and frameworks are a necessary place to start in building a network. These first steps feel a bit touchy-feely. And for you crazy data people that demand measurable outcomes—more power to you—here we go!

**RR REFLECTION**

Schools across the network are using the ACT college readiness instruments in similar ways and sharing how they are loading and using their data to help place freshman students in the right courses.

## Metrics

When we say that new strategies are producing results for kids, how do

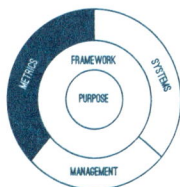

we know? We know because we are committed to a common set of measurement tools that work inside every high school regardless of model. These tools are a set of national metrics that create a national assessment infrastructure. Without these metrics, the framework and stories might as well be told in a barbershop. The network schools are committed to a common set of measurable outcomes for students. Below is the assessment strategy aligned to the College Acceleration Network framework, which is the same framework as the research high school.

## ⓇⓇ REFLECTION

We already have some good instruments that are linked to college and workplace success. It takes a whole lot of money and time to build new instruments. That money could be better allocated in building the technology and data system infrastructure that high schools require to innovate together.

If research high schools are the perfect place for groups to begin to try new instruments and tools to measure college and workplace readiness, and if these practices show promise, they can be documented and sent quickly through the network. Infrastructure is a beautiful thing!

It is important to explain one thing before we dig into the instruments. Many talented people are working all over the country on new assessment tools and models. What most people want is existing practical tools that they can use right now. Our kids deserve this as well. Below you will notice that each part of the framework has instruments listed. These instruments are essential to measure the success or failure of school-based programs and strategies.

The measurement instruments are non-negotiable in the network. These instruments drive results-management in all the network schools. Schools that join the network are supported by beginning the assessment processes based on their needs and ability to afford the tools. These existing strong tools help measure the twenty-first century skills our students need to

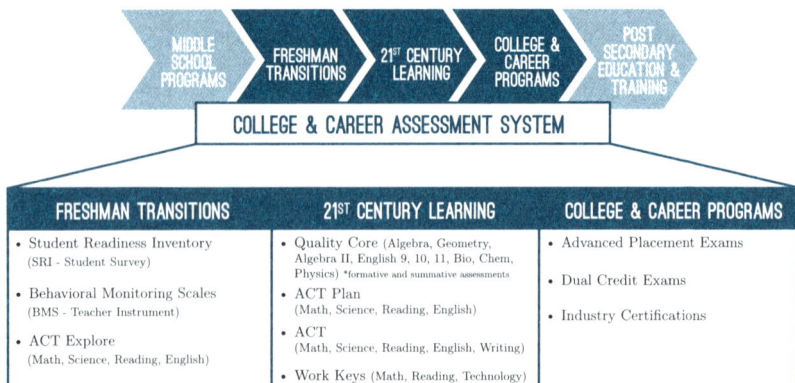

| MIDDLE SCHOOL PROGRAMS | FRESHMAN TRANSITIONS | 21ˢᵀ CENTURY LEARNING | COLLEGE & CAREER PROGRAMS | POST SECONDARY EDUCATION & TRAINING |

### COLLEGE & CAREER ASSESSMENT SYSTEM

| FRESHMAN TRANSITIONS | 21ˢᵀ CENTURY LEARNING | COLLEGE & CAREER PROGRAMS |
|---|---|---|
| • Student Readiness Inventory (SRI - Student Survey) | • Quality Core (Algebra, Geometry, Algebra II, English 9, 10, 11, Bio, Chem, Physics) *formative and summative assessments | • Advanced Placement Exams |
| • Behavioral Monitoring Scales (BMS - Teacher Instrument) | • ACT Plan (Math, Science, Reading, English) | • Dual Credit Exams |
| • ACT Explore (Math, Science, Reading, English) | • ACT (Math, Science, Reading, English, Writing) | • Industry Certifications |
| | • Work Keys (Math, Reading, Technology) | |

be competitive in a global economy. These metrics are valued by the cooperating workforce and post-secondary partners. Let's do a little walk through of the metrics.

***Freshman transition:*** These national metrics are designed and administered during the middle school years to measure the academic achievement (critical thinking) levels and the academic behaviors (twenty-first century workplace skills) that are required for a strong transition into high school. High schools partner with middle schools to help build pathways and interventions using this data. High schools then measure students again on the same skills at the end of the freshman year to measure growth and development.

***Twenty-first century learning:*** These national metrics are designed to measure college and workforce readiness. Some tools are course-based tools (like chemistry formative and summative assessments) and others are longitudinal tools like the ACT and Work Keys. All of these tools provide data to ensure accountability through the system.

***College and career programming:*** These are a combination of national and regional tools. Advanced Placement is a long-tested assessment approach that has national currency for college credit. Common dual credit exams can be implemented from a state or national perspective. Or, as in our case, they can be implemented with regional campuses addressing the needs of the regional workforce. Industry certifications are a combination of national, state, and regional certification exams that provide students currency and drive accountability through the workforce-focused programs in high school.

Common metrics in the system are critical. Schools have a host of other metrics that are used for a variety of programming decisions that are outside of the network tools. Again, the purpose of the network tools is to advocate for a common set of college and career acceleration metrics to measure performance and drive stronger results and innovation. An entire book could be written on mapping out the assessment plan. On our infrastructure tour, this was scheduled to be a brief stop.

### *Systems*

Common frameworks and assessments produce a ton of data. This data has to be managed at the national, state, regional, district, school, teacher, and student levels. A new set of data management tools is in development to support the data management needs of everyone in the pipeline. There are two systems that work in combination to help network schools communicate, plan, make decisions, and improve together. The first is reporting tools and the second is learning management tools.

*Reporting tools:* Most current high school reporting tools are disconnected from the pragmatic needs of many inside and outside of the system. For example, much of the data we generate and send to the state has questionable value to our industry leaders who are looking for some simple and specific information on emerging employees. Imagine for a moment that we had one common high school transcript that actually served everyone in the system. In our mission to better prepare students for college and careers, what if this transcript actually resulted in improved behavior and performance from parents and students? What would be on this transcript? I don't think that is very difficult to answer if you ask yourself what people value. Here are some common values of the workforce and post-secondary institutions:

→ Attendance: Do they show up for work on time everyday?

→ Standardized test scores and grades: Can they think and solve problems?

→ Student Activities: Do they work well with others?

→ Community Service: Are they a caring member of a community?

I just listed a few things that are low hanging fruit. We have all this data. We just don't have it in a place and format where it is useful to most people. In our region, we are driving conversations about the information that will transform the pipeline of fourteen to eighteen-year-olds by placing them in a competitive regional system where college, training, and jobs are the goals.

**RR REFLECTION**

State departments of education can be a big player in driving the right systems for this work. They have influence over data and can influence districts to adopt a common platform.

I talk with vendors all the time who drive the work the wrong way. Every vendor wants you to drive on their proprietary learning system. The more we do this, the more the data becomes disconnected. We can't serve kids and families well unless we have a strong technology and integration strategy that drives valuable vendors to a common system.

The unique aspect of our emerging tools is the way in which we are piecing the entire picture together to provide everyone in the system with data that will make them more effective. The data will actually cascade to serve the needs of everyone in the system. The following are the foundational questions that drove the development of a new set of reporting tools:

| Reporting Tools for: | Accountability | Growth / Support |
|---|---|---|
| *Student / Parent* | *Where am I compared to others?* | *What can I do to accelerate my growth?* |

| Teacher | Where am I compared to others? | What can I do to accelerate the growth of my students? |
|---|---|---|
| High School | Where are we compared to others? | What can we do accelerate the growth of groups of students? |
| District | Where are we compared to others? | What can we do in the K-12 system to better position students to successfully enter high school? |
| Region | Where are we compared to other regions? What are workforce readiness trends? What are college readiness trends? | What can we do to support more schools to produce better results? |
| State | Where are we compared to other states? | What policies and practices will best support this work? |
| Nation / International | What can we do as a country to regain our position as number one in college completion? | What policies and practices will best support this work? |

**Learning tools:** Ultimately, teachers are like physicians who need the right data at the right time to make decisions about learning. As part of the infrastructure plan, a common system, or groups of systems, will be required to more effectively flow the data to the people in the system at the right time to make decisions. Also, these systems will help to package content, align work to the right standards, manage real-time assessment information, and allow everyone in the system to be linked by common interests and experiences to help drive improvement faster.

In a recent conversation with a neighboring school district, they requested that we help them to deliver a medical terminology course that we are offering through Indiana University Northwest (IUN). We took the IUN digital course and packaged it in the BrainHoney learning system. The neighbor district has planned to move to the same learning system. All we will have to do is flip a switch, and, bingo, our course is now their course.

In a recent conversation with a different neighbor school district, we began collaboratively planning to build common formative assessments with ACT inside our emerging common digital courses to accelerate the growth of our freshman students in the core academic areas like English, algebra, biology, and world history. We are both interested in managing the college acceleration growth by providing our teachers with clear and powerful three-week reports by course, class, and student. These reports are to be used by course-based team leaders to plan real-time instruction and interventions to meet the needs of our students. Using the same learning system and same reports has dramatically reduced the development costs to each of us and provides external networks of teachers that can support one another.

In a recent conversation with still a different neighboring school district, we planned our dual credit work together. Once again, our model requires high school students to take the same midterm and final exams as the on-campus students. The neighboring high school is forming the same university relationship and will be moving to the same learning system so our teachers of the same course (like college composition) can work together and support one another in effectively managing the assessment and reporting process. We have invested and built one inter-rater scoring technology that is now available to all schools in the network.

## ⓇⓇ REFLECTION

Reflection: All these examples are emerging in an organic way. There are a finite number of common things we need to do, like offer dual credit, administer assessments, and run reports. The more we are on the same learning system, the simpler it will be to help one another.

You may be asking, "What is the role of the research high school in the network?" That is a great question. In the early work, we have just been a resource to help high schools think about the what: assessments, learning systems, and strategies like dual credit. Ideally, we would like to have a stronger role in working with regional economic development and add some research staff to work on some critical questions for the region. We aspire to truly become the R&D arm for human capital development for the region.

Currently we are able to convene, share, and provide examples and support. As we attract investment, we are beginning to help districts manage high school data to improve student outcomes.

There are dozens more examples of our regional network of high schools collaborating to make our work more efficient and effective through running programming on the same learning system. This learning system will be linked to the reporting system to help all the data flow seamlessly throughout the region. Business leaders will be blown away when they see the regional transparency on college and workforce skill development across all high schools. This idea is so simple and so effective in better serving our regional needs cheaper, better, and faster.

### Management of Data

Managing data and systems across a region or state is no walk in the park. I truly respect our Indiana Department of Education's capacity to manage oceans of data and reports from districts. Since the network is emerging, and infrastructure is the key to success in helping schools, regions, and the state manage better college and workforce readiness results, let's review who needs to do what.

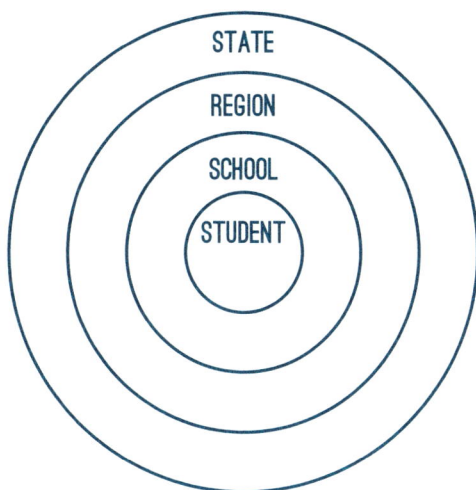

At the center of the work is the individual student. Their trajectories are the most important focus for a college and career readiness system. Students and parents must have the tools to manage their own trajectories, and it is our job in schools to provide those tools and support. Schools are next with data on individual student and groups of students. We will use the data from the same instruments. This data is used here to sort groups of students to see what programs and activities best support their growth. Regions need to look at groups of students across schools to understand what profiles and types of students are being best served. Finally, the state needs to look at schools growth in relation to the targets established to make judgments on account-ability and performance. If all the metrics are the same and everyone in the system is playing on the same page (learning system), then the work becomes much more connected, relevant, and manageable.

> + State Policy: Define the new and simple metrics for accountability and learning system for the state. Require schools to provide comprehensive information to populate a state high school transcript.

> → Region Focus: Promote the use of the state metrics and learning system to support schools and help transition more students into regional colleges, post-secondary training, and the workplace.

> → School Use: Every teacher and administrator embraces the state metrics and learning system to drive performance at the building and department level, and instruction and learning at the teacher, and student level.

> → Student Value: Every student and parent use real-time data to recognize the current levels of achievement through a new enhanced online data system that provides more relevant information for college entry and workplace preparation.

If all the circles align, we end up with a laser-focused picture for every high school student (the common transcript), then everyone in the system has a fighting chance to manage the data to produce the results we need. If these stars do not align, then we all will have a difficult data management road ahead.

This chapter provided the conditions for management but not the specific management solutions. I propose putting the horse before the cart. Infrastructure is the first step. There is no clean data management unless there are common metrics and systems. The research high school will be a vehicle for "how" to help regions and network schools manage data and results.

Purpose, frameworks, metrics, systems, and management are the key elements of a new college and career information infrastructure that is well positioned to drive innovation and economic development across a region. I recognize the challenge we face in our current political environment to drive these concepts to completion. But once we do, and we produce big results, I will write a second book on how to manage a network of schools producing stronger college and workforce results for kids.

# CHAPTER NINE

REGIONAL ECONOMIC DEVELOPMENT: A CASE STUDY

*"No problem can be solved from the same level*
*of consciousness that created it."*

ALBERT EINSTEIN.

Too often in education, we ask the people that created the problem to solve it. Further, we see school boards change, superintendents change, high school principals change, and yet we get frustrated that we don't have the collective movement we need to get things going in the right direction.

Let's allow ourselves the time and opportunity to fly through a region. We start our flight over the urban areas, where you find dysfunctional politics and poverty that lead to mind boggling issues, from absent parents and student dropouts to gangs and a constant struggle just to manage student behavior. Partner that with the struggle to attract the best people in education, and a shallow minority teacher applicant pool, and you have one tough deal. Now blast out of the inner city and jet through the mix of urban and suburban environments that are managing a changing student population faced with issues like disengaged middle track students, drugs, and new and diverse family backgrounds. Now we enter suburbia airspace, the most confident place in American culture, where everything is wonderful, and don't you don't dare hear anything other than "We Rock!" and "No Child Left Behind isn't going to label

us!" This confidence fuels the workers on the factory floor to resist change—
"Why do we need to change how we do business?" Now glide over the hills to
wide open green space, out to the rural places, where small schools struggle to
provide the programming that is essential for students to be competitive.

We recognize and respect that regions possess complex high school environments that have different challenges in preparing all students for college and
the workplace. These unique high school environments are under considerable
financial stress with ever increasing accountability and expectations. A former
entrepreneurial boss used to say despair spelled opportunity. Now more than
ever, high schools are looking for ways to reduce costs, serve students well, and
meet the changing demands of the twenty-first century global economy. As you
have learned from the examples and systems presented in this book, there is a
real opportunity to drive sustainable improvements through infrastructure. So
how do we pull this together in a region and what could it look like?

This chapter is a case study to examine the work of the research high
school and the regional network high schools in the context of regional economic development. This chapter outlines some bold ideas that are emerging
in Northwest Indiana, an economic region built on the steel industry. The
Northwest Indiana economy is moving from an industrial machine to a global
advanced manufacturing leader. This global movement, called "One Region
One Vision" will succeed primarily because of the plan to embrace the transformation of Northwest Indiana high schools.

### *The Real Investors*

Over two years ago the Center for Excellence in Learning Leadership
(CELL) at the University of Indianapolis sent a senior advisor (and the for-

mer executive director of CELL) to Northwest Indiana to meet with a team of industry leaders. The agenda was regional economic development and high schools. I was fortunate to be at this meeting. I clearly saw, heard, and felt the scars participants described from all the past attempts at reinventing our regional high schools. They tried everything under the sun with a sincere commitment that included time, talent, and treasure.

It became abundantly clear to me that this group of industry leaders was the critical piece of the regional accountability picture.

## REGIONAL EFFORTS

These leaders represented law, steel, energy, development, construction, and tourism. They described in detail the money and time they invested in urban high school reform work. They brought in Six Sigma teams, implemented Baldrige Management Models and other processes. All these efforts and initiatives did not seem to move the dial towards improvement. As you would expect, the business leaders were not really motivated to throw money or time at another idea.

They were the regional group that had the longest-term investment in our future. They had outlasted every principal and superintendent. So you can understand why they were also a tough sell with new ideas like a research high school and regional network. CELL has a powerful approach to partnering with regional economic development to influence and drive change in high schools. They have a long track record of success, but just as our industry leaders have discovered, CELL has also discovered that long-term capacity building is an almost insurmountable challenge without some new structural innovations. CELL has come to learn that if one key person departs from a region, the system most often reverts back to the old status quo quicker than a rocking chair on the front porch of a Cracker Barrel restaurant.

## The Summit

Northwest Indiana is fortunate to have a workforce development leader who is committed and determined to drive improvements across the region. Over two years of work with CELL, industry leaders, workforce development, higher education, high schools, and media produced the "One Region One Vision" summit to revitalize high schools. This summit was a first of its kind in our region.

It is important to understand the context of urban and suburban sprawl in Northwest Indiana. There is no mayor, no one group with ultimate authority, and no gorilla in the room apart from the steel industry. We have towns and cities that all border one another. It is tough work to bring this region together. With over two years of hard work convening groups, the summit attracted every leader in K-12, post-secondary, workforce development, and industry. The summit was headlined by the Undersecretary of education, Martha Kanter, and she was blown away by the focus and organization that Northwest Indiana demonstrated. Our regional leaders constructed a powerful summit and compact to launch a new structure for regional economic development that would hold high schools more accountable than ever, and at the same time provide a level of support they never experienced. The compact that was signed by every leader in the region is provided below.

### Northwest Indiana Partnership Compact

**Vision:** Northwest Indiana will need a twenty-first century workforce in order for the community to thrive in this global economy. To achieve this vision, 100 percent of our students graduating from high school must possess the knowledge, skills and habits of mind required for success in post-secondary education, the military, apprenticeships, or employment.

Leaders from Jasper, Lake, La Porte, Newton, Porter, Pulaski and Starke Counties—The Northwest Indiana Partnership—will build this regional workforce aligned with and respectful of each community's needs for access, support, and sustainability.

The initial phase of this plan will begin implementation in 2011-2012 and will focus on annual student growth metrics, grades nine through fourteen.

***Mission:*** The Northwest Indiana Partnership commits to regional thinking and acting, and the need to ensure prosperity throughout the entire area while supporting the unique aspects of community, school, and student. NIP partners are businesses, K-12, post-secondary and proprietary schools, labor, government, non-profits and community leaders committed to connect the education of youth with post-secondary college and career outcomes aligned with regional economic and civic growth.

***Goal:*** To expand implementation of programs in Northwest Indiana which already have proven results. To closely measure these programs to assure that these concepts can be used more broadly with a high probability of helping students in high school prepare for a successful and productive career in the workplace. To utilize measurement techniques for monitoring the progress students make in reaching the goal of readiness for the workplace and the success of a system allowing dual credit for students interested in receiving college credit for work accomplished in high school whether those credits lead to a two-year or a four-year degree.

The Partnership roles and responsibilities include the following:

### Business and Labor

- → Influence state policy to have metrics in high schools that align to our actual goal of college and career readiness

- → Commit to public reporting of college and career readiness information

- → Promote progress and results

- → Invest in promising/proven strategies aligned with progress and results

- → Invest in the NIP network or a supporting initiative such as the Work-Keys pilot

## K-12

- → High schools and districts commit to measuring actual college and workforce readiness and use twenty-first century learning system (Indiana College Acceleration Network, or ICAN)

- → Share data and resources

- → Commit project management and resources to meet routinely—disciplined and sustained meetings using shared data to make informed decisions

## Post-Secondary

- → Commit to further rollout of dual credit—commit to number of schools and set the pre-conditions for those schools

- → Expand on-line instruction for high school dual credit and other innovative teaching and learning delivery modes

- → Continue to focus on teamwork, critical thinking, communication and problem solving skills for students

## Workforce and Economic Development

- → Communicate career opportunities broadly aligned with labor market

- → Provide more field experiences and internships to support students and businesses and schools

- → Support regional promising and proven practices

## Community

- → Develop understanding of and provide student support for achieving college and workforce competencies

- → Provide mentoring opportunities for students

- → Stay engaged and stay informed on progress of students and outcomes being achieved in local school system

As a follow up to the summit, the undersecretary returned six months later for a back to school launch with the U.S. Secretary of Education Arne Duncan and the Indiana State School Superintendent of Instruction Tony Bennett. This event sponsored by the Times Media Group again convened over 600 business and education leaders in the region.

Business and education leaders began to feel the movement and opportunity. They have great instincts on where to invest their time and money. They recognized the commitment of the region and began to more powerfully embrace this work. After two years of work, I began to see a glimmer in their eye. I knew the look as a fellow hunter. They recognized the opportunity. It was time to think about a powerful new structure to drive innovation and results in the region. It was time to invest in high schools to drive a stronger economy. After talking with many regional industry leaders they understood the following progression and talked about it with me. I just documented their words in the following graphic.

R&D → HUMAN CAPITAL → NEW COMPANIES → STRONGER ECONOMY/ REGION → NEW REVENUE

### The Structure

We moved from the summit and commitments from every stakeholder on our regional compact into action. The big question was how do we build sustainability to drive consistent long-term change in high schools? We continued to meet and discuss the concept of how do we embrace the two powerful concepts of the research high school and infrastructure to best serve the region. While we wrestled with this idea, superintendents and principals began to meet and work on the infrastructure planning. There was a critical mass of

## THE REGIONAL MOVEMENT

Dozens of high schools began to join the movement. The exciting part is that the framework for improvement applied to all high schools. Every school told their unique story through freshman transitions, twenty-first century learning, and college and career programming.

Urban schools, suburban, rural, small learning communities, academies, new tech highs—we all began to align to the work.

schools and leaders moving forward together. High schools were building brochures together that used the research high school framework; superintendents were inviting senior management from ACT to Northwest Indiana to learn about college and workforce readiness instruments. As the region buzzed with educational leaders moving hard into relevant work in alignment with our regional compact, we had to think quickly about the structure that would support this work. Meeting as a regional economic development and education team, we

realized that we had to invest in research high school personnel to support the innovation work and build a regional structure outside of existing school structures. This external structure would ensure that schools were supported when they hit walls and were celebrated when they posted wins. This structure would advance an agenda of college and workforce readiness and use some carrots and sticks to get high schools moving. The network would operate outside of school districts and be funded initially by a regional economic development grant to implement the regional compact. The regional structure had oversight by a regional economic development board, which supported new personnel and worked to develop regional college and workforce goals and research agendas with the research high school site. As network high schools joined, they were provided incentives, tools, and technical support to help drive regional goals.

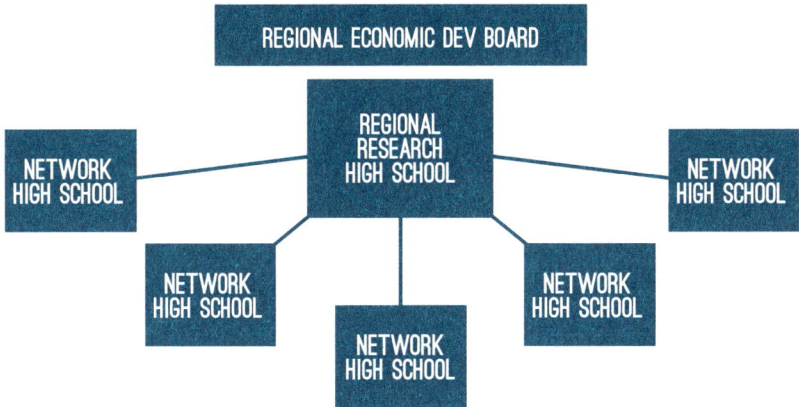

## ICAN: The Indiana College Acceleration Network

The Indiana College Acceleration Network was born from the commitments of the courageous industry leaders from Northwest Indiana who understood the importance of high schools in the economic development future of the region. The network embraces the two breakthrough ideas presented in this book. First, the regional research high school is funded through investments, district contributions, and grants to support the required personnel to work on research and development. Second, the regional economic development board is leading the creation of the right infrastructure by influencing state and local policy, securing investments, and providing incentives and resources for districts to engage in the work. Today, the "One Region One Vision" compact is being boldly enacted through the work of regional industry leaders, post-secondary partners, high schools, parents, and students.

# PERSPECTIVE

*"Rarely do we find men who willingly engage in hard, solid thinking. There is an almost universal quest for easy answers and half-baked solutions. Nothing pains some people more than having to think."*

REV. MARTIN LUTHER KING, JR.

On the thirty-ninth floor of the Petroleum Club in Dallas, I often had lunch with visiting educational leaders who were making things happen in the field. I really admired and respected their work and focus. They were committed to producing results from the ground floor. I enjoy being on the ground floor now. It has been awesome (and tough work) to drive innovation from within the system. The system is tough and resilient. The factory floor I step onto every day in many ways operates as it did at the turn of the century. Even though we have made strong progress in many areas, we have bells that ring every fifty minutes, we move 2,600 students seven times a day, we have ratio of thirty kids for one teacher in each period, and they sit in desks. We, like many schools, are planning and implementing a one-to-one environment where we will re-tool the "factory floor" to better deliver on the learning vision of the twenty-first century.

I have great hope that our one-to-one environment will be running on a new regional and state infrastructure to drive transformational practices and results. One initiative underway is the development of collegeacceleration.com. I will conclude with the three big steps for transformation for the American public high school. It will take the vision, commitment, and talent of leaders to follow these steps (and lead the world in educational infrastructure development, R & D, and networking). In the end, these steps will reconstruct high schools to power economic development.

### Step 1: Build the Infrastructure (State Department of Education)

↗ Common Transcript: Construct a common state high school transcript with the right college and workforce metrics that will serve the needs of everyone in the K-16 system. Define the data that districts must routinely submit to the state department of education, and then build a viewable marketing transcript that students, parents, teachers, administrators, employers, military, and post-secondary institutions and trade schools can use as currency to spend.

↗ Common Dashboards: Develop dashboards for state accountability (state), school transformation (region and school), instructional improvement (teacher), and individual educational planning (student and parent) based on the common instruments and information.

↗ Common Learning System: Adopt a state learning system that provides teachers and students course-based formative assessment items, dual credit exams, and digital content. If teachers embrace the use of common assessments in a common learning system, teaching practices that produce results will be more transparent and transferrable. In the end more teachers will produce better results for the real beneficiaries, the kids.

## Step 2: Invest in R&D (Regional Economic Development)

→ Identify research high school site(s) based on current results and the strength of the district leadership, stable school board, and rock star high school administrative team and faculty. I would recommend that an outside group come in to evaluate the potential sites.

→ Invest in the following roles for the research high school:

**Research Administrator:** The research high school requires a research administrator in addition to the high school principal. This administrator reports to both the superintendent and the regional economic development board. The research agenda is co-constructed for the research high school to serve the community and the region. One major role of the research high school administrator is to organize and manage the external partnerships required to serve fourteen to eighteen-year-olds for the region. These include universities, community colleges, trade schools, workforce development offices, and community agencies.

- Develop regional college and workforce goals for fourteen to eighteen-year-olds
- Develop regional research agenda with a network of interested schools
- Manage research high school demonstration site(s) and regional high school study groups
- Implement regional communication plan
- Deliver regional training within and across the state
- Provide support to implementing network high schools

*Data Communication Management:* This role organizes data, reporting, and communication processes for the research high school and all schools in the network.

- Manage data systems for the regional network of high schools
- Provide data support for network high schools
- Develop reporting protocols for all stakeholders

*Research Faculty (Instructional Coaches):* The research high school requires a team of professionals who have the time and training to ask questions and drive new practice.

- Define new practices as a master teacher
- Manage assigned research questions
- Coach teachers as a team leader on data and instruction
- Present new practices and results
- Publish new practices and results
- Develop blended trainings, online, and face-to-face to support network schools
- Annually evaluate research high school program progress and tools produced for dissemination and evaluate fidelity of network high school adoption and adaptations of research high school work

*Step 3: Connect The High Schools: The College Acceleration Network (Regional Economic Development)*

↝ Ensure that every high school in the region becomes a network school linked to the regional R&D site(s) to drive innovation through the region and compete with other regions to see which region has:

- The highest percentage of college and career ready graduates.

- Hits the Lumina Foundation's big goal of 60% of the population with high quality post-secondary credentials and degrees by 2025.

I hold great hope for the future of the American public high school. These three steps constitute the strongest initial strides toward building sustainable improvement and transformation in America's high schools. They are solid in thinking, theory, and practice. They provide the foundation for talented high school leaders to help America reclaim a position of excellence in the new world economy. I ask you to avoid the urge to buy the quick fix, jet pack at the trade show. Rather, consider a long-term sustainable investment in infrastructure. In our history, that choice has clearly been the difference in this country's position in the world economy. We are indebted to a former president for having the courage to act on a vision of a connected and sustainable United States. I admire leaders who have the courage to think!

*"Together, the united forces of our communication and transportation systems are dynamic elements in the very name we bear—United States. Without them, we would be a mere alliance of many separate parts."*

IN REFERENCE TO BUILDING THE INTERSTATE HIGHWAY SYSTEM.

PRESIDENT DWIGHT D. EISENHOWER

FEBRUARY 22, 1955

# ACKNOWLEDGEMENTS

I would like to thank my incredible wife Karen and my kids Oscar, Brick, and Mae. Your love, support, and energy are an inspiration. I love you!

I dedicate this book to the just in time intellectual network of great thinkers and hunters that challenge me to be better in everything I do. I have worked as a teacher next to you, I have sat in your classes, we have worked to develop programs, we have built products, we have taken risks, failed, learned, persisted, and ultimately succeeded in producing huge results like any good team!

Specifically, I have a few folks to thank (I will call you coaches):

- Leonard Burrello, my intellectual coach
- John Ban, my writing coach
- Randy Best, my entrepreneurial coach
- Nancy Sutton, my political coach
- Jeri Nowakowski, my curriculum coach
- Teresa Eineman, my public education coach

Finally, I would like to thank the community of Crown Point. We sit and talk with candor to challenge one another to build stronger programming so all students achieve beyond their potential. This is the foundation of the research high school. I am proud to serve with you!